SUMMARY REPORT

OF

JOHN K. HOWARD

AND

H. WENDELL ENDICOTT

Representatives of

The Massachusetts Committee on Public Safety

The State House

Boston, Massachusetts

RE

The Home Guard (British)

*Based on an investigation made by Messrs.
Howard and Endicott in England, February
14th to March 25th, 1941.*

This report is of a confidential nature and is to be made available only to such authorities as may be designated by the War Department at Washington, and the Massachusetts Committee on Public Safety.

This copy is Number 256

Issued to Gen. R. E. Lee
Ass't. Chief of Staff G-2
War Dept. Washington

Signed H Wendell Endicott

Dated: Feb 13th 1942

Published by Books Express Publishing
Copyright © Books Express, 2010
ISBN 978-1-907521-41-6
To purchase copies at discounted prices please contact
info@books-express.com

INDEX

	PAGE
Foreword	1
Partial List of People Interviewed	3

PART ONE INTRODUCTION

Section A—OCCASION 5
    Comment by Sir Edward Grigg 5

Section B—RECENT HISTORY INDICATING MILITARY NECESSITY OF SUCH A FORCE AS THE BRITISH HOME GUARD 5
    Comment by General Sir Alan Brooke 5
        (1) Spain 6
        (2) Poland 6
        (3) Norway 6
        (4) Holland 6
        (5) Belgium and France 7
    Force Similar to Home Guard Necessary 7
    Official Opinions on the Importance of the Home Guard 8

Section C—HISTORY 8
    Picture before English People May 1940 8
    Birth of the Home Guard May 14th, 1940 9
    Conception
        Statement by Tom Wintringham 9
    German Reaction 10
    Status 10
    Early Sporadic Movements of Local Defence 10
    History of Organization 10
    Responsibility in Army Council 11
    Help from Police 11
    Inspector General of L.D.V. 11
    Appointment of Home Guard Directorate 11
    Osterly Park School for Home Guard Instruction 11
    General Eastwood as Director General of Home Guard 12
    Territorial Associations 12
    L. D. V. Training Instruction No. 1, May 1940 13
    Army Council Instructions June 24, 1940 13

	PAGE
Name of the Force changed from L.D.V. to Home Guard July 1940	13
Home Guard a Force of 1,750,000	14

SPIRIT AND MORALE 14

    All Classes Volunteer for Home Guard 14

    Comment by General Eastwood 14

    Ex-High Ranking Officers Now Soldiers in Home Guard 15

    Everybody a Worker 15

    Comments by J.K.H. and H.W.E. 15

    Morale: Effect of Home Guard on Population 16

    Comments by General Eastwood 16

    Comments by Lt. Colonel Sir Thomas Moore, M.P. 16

    Comments by Colonel Ebenezer Pike 16

    Comments by General Sir Cecil Romer 17

    Comments by Mr. Lawson, M.P. 17

    Comments by Major Lord Denham 17

PART TWO—TACTICS AND TRAINING

    Section D—TACTICS 18

        Early Conception 18

        Defence of Strong Points 18

        The Three Tactical Functions 18

        Warning 19

        Delaying 19

        Delaying (Defensive Positions) 19

        Delaying (Nodal Points) 19

        Factories 19

        Towns and Cities 20

        Delaying ("Scorched Earth" Mission) 20

        Duty as Guides 20

        Harassing 20

        Arms 21

    Section E—TRAINING

        Organization 21

        Director Military Training 21

        Command and Area Staff Officers 21

	PAGE
General Training—Unit Commanders	
Regular Army Cooperation	21
Permanent Staff Instructors	22
Area and Sub-Area School	22
Training Publications	22
General Training	22
Drill	23
Guard Duty	23
Observation and Reporting of Information	24
Weapon Training	25
The Rifle	26
Anti-Aircraft Fire	26
The Browning Automatic Rifle	27
The Thompson Sub-Machine Gun	28
The Light Machine Gun	28
Machine Guns	28
Grenades and Bombs	30
The Bayonet	31
The Pistol and Revolver	32
Use of Flame—Fougasse	32
Land Mines and Tank Traps	33
Booby Traps	33
First Aid	34
Gas	34
Fieldcraft	35
Training by Lectures, etc.	36
Training by Exercises	37
Concealment and Camouflage	37
Training by Lectures	38
Training by Exercises	38
Field Fortifications	38
Tactical Training	40
Minor Tactics	40
Special Tactical Role	41

	PAGE
Anti-Air Troops	41
Tank Destruction	43
Tank Hunting	44
Tank Destruction—Passive Phase	44
Road Blocks	45
Village Defense	51
Comment by Langdon-Davies	51
Comment by Wintringham	51
Instructions	52
Principles	53
Control of Civilians—Shortt	54
Anti-Aircraft	54
Factory Defense	54
Factory Units—Ryley	55
Official Instructions	56
General Role	56
Control of Employees	56
Scheme of Defense	57
Guerrilla Warfare	58
By Lectures and Pamphlets	59
By Exercises	60
Guides	60
Special Jobs	62
Control of Civilian Population	62
Bomb Reconnaissance	63
PART THREE—LAW AND ORGANIZATION	64
Section F—AUTHORITY FOR HOME GUARD	64
Section G—LEGAL STATUS OF MEMBERS OF HOME GUARD	64
At International Law	64
At Military Law	64
At Civil Law	64
Powers, Rights and Duties under Certain Acts	65
Section H—ORGANIZATION	66
Army Council	66

	PAGE
War Office	66
Chain of Command "Regular" Forces	66
Home Guard Units and Commanders	67
Chains of Operational Command—Home Guard	67
Chain of Control for Training Purposes	68
Chain of Control for Administration and Supply	68
Tables of Organization	68
Home Guard Officers	68
Rank	69
Appointive Authority	69
Precedence	69
Qualifications	69
Commissions	70
Essential Differences	70
Continuity	70
Resignations and Terminations	70
Home Guard Warrant Officers and N.C.O.'s	70
Appointive Authority	71
Resignations and Terminations	71
Enrollment of Members of Home Guard	71
Conditions	71
Procedure	72
Extensions	72
Transfers	72
Discharges	72
Documents and Records	72
Identity Card	72
Periodic Orders	72
Casualties	72
Medical	73
Discipline	73
Complaints	73
Press Communications	73
	73

	PAGE
Adjutant—Quartermaster Officers	73
Administrative Assistants	74
Clerical Assistants	74
Permanent Staff Instructors	74
Telephones	74
Financial Grant	74
Uniform, Equipment, etc.	75
Insignia of Rank	75
Arms and Ammunition	75
Engineer and Ordnance Stores	76
Accounting	76
Offices, Drill Halls, etc.	76
Travel Allowances	76
Use of Unlicensed Cars	76
Automobile Insurance	77
Subsistence	77
Disablement Allowance	77
Pensions	78
Pensions to Widows	78
Children's Pensions and Allowances	78
Life Insurance	79
Maintenance of Families	79
Funeral Expenses	79
Scheme of Compensation for War Damage	79
PART FOUR—PITFALLS AND CONCLUSIONS	80
Section I—PITFALLS	80
Section J—CONCLUSIONS	82
BIBLIOGRAPHY	86

FOREWORD

With the complete cooperation of the American Embassy, the British War Office in London, and particularly the Home Guard Directorate of the War Office, we were given every opportunity to pursue our studies of the Home Guard in all its phases. Interviews were arranged with various military officers and statesmen of England. Interviews were also arranged with officers and statesmen of foreign countries who were then in London and who had been through the campaigns of Poland, Norway, Holland, Belgium, France and Spain, with the object that we might have first hand information about their plans of defense or omissions in defense, particularly as they related to the value of or necessity for such a force as the Home Guard.

In pursuing our studies of this general subject we sought to interview those people whose opinions would be valuable. This meant not only several statesmen in high positions, but commanding officers of greater or lesser rank, as well as men in the ranks.

NOTE: Following this foreword is a partial list of those we interviewed.

We were further given the opportunity of attending the full course at the War Office School No. 1. This is a school for Home Guard instructors. In a six-day concentrated course it specializes on the theory and tactics of modern warfare, particularly as introduced by the enemy. It describes as well the weapons used in such tactics and the ways and means of meeting such tactics.

Our studies also included inspection of the actual organizations and their training activities in cities, towns, villages and on moors, in areas from the Channel Coast to the cities in the northwest. Our work further included the collection of evidence of the psychology and morale of the Home Guard force, as well as its status and its importance in the plans of defense of the country, documented by official and other publications. Our work further required the collecting of such official orders, "Instructions" and War Office pamphlets and other official and recommended data as had a bearing on the organization and training of this Force.

It is obvious that on the completion of our studies in England our first job was an intelligent analysis of this material. Our second job was the preparation of an exhaustive and complete report in detail with appendices, exhibits, photographs, etc. It would have been possible to throw together a hastily prepared report with a mass of material improperly arranged and organized, but that, as we saw it, was not the object of our mission. We have, however, completed our first job, namely the "digestive process."

The study of defense in the United States today is being given greater and greater thought. Accordingly we feel at this time that it would be proper and timely to submit to the War Department, and the Massachusetts Committee on Public Safety, a "Summary Report" which gives the essence of the Home Guard in the British Isles, hence this tentative, or as it might better be termed "Summary Report."

An examination of the Index will give a summary of subjects covered by this report. The "Conclusions," Part Four, Section J, page 82, give a summarization of the report.

The main and detailed report is in preparation.

JOHN K. HOWARD
H. WENDELL ENDICOTT

June, 1941

NOTE: The original printing of this Summary Report consisted of 100 copies numbered in sequence. The second printing of which this is a copy consists of 300 copies numbered consecutively from 101 to 400 inclusive. The second printing was undertaken to meet the request for a broader distribution under official authorization. In this reprint certain typographical errors have been corrected and several minor changes made.

PARTIAL LIST OF PEOPLE INTERVIEWED ON OUR MISSION IN ENGLAND

Mr. Edward Margesson, *Secretary of State for War*

Mr. Brendon Bracken, M.P., 10 Downing Street, *Parliamentary Secretary of Mr. Winston Churchill*

General Sir Alan Brooke, *Commander-in-Chief of all the British Forces in the British Isles*

Lt. General T. R. Eastwood, C.B., D.S.O., M.C., *Director General of the Home Guard*

General Viscount Robert Bridgeman, *Deputy Director of the Home Guard*

Lt. Colonel Gerald Elias-Morgan, *Assistant Director of the Home Guard*

Sir Edward Grigg, *Joint Under-Secretary of State for War*

Major General L. D. Hickes, *Director of Staff Duties (Weapons), War Office*

General James Whitehead, *Home Guard Commander, London District*

Colonel Peter Shortt, *G.S.O. 1, Military Training Home Guard (M.T.7)*

Lt. Colonel J. D. Carlisle, *Directorate of Military Intelligence, War Office*

Lt. Colonel Sir Harold Wernher, *Liaison Officer, Southeastern Command Staff, Home Guard*

Major Lord Denham, *Liaison Officer, London District Command Staff, Home Guard*

General A. W. Purser, *Liaison Officer, Western Command Staff, Home Guard*

General Sir Cecil Romer, *Special Adviser to Home Guard*

Lt. Colonel H. A. Pollock, *Commandant War Office School Number One*

Mr. Thomas Wintringham, *War Office School Number One, Officer International Brigade Spanish Civil War*

Mr. Hugh Slater, *War Office School Number One, Late Chief of Operations International Brigade Staff Spanish Civil War*

Lt. Colonel B. C. T. Paget, C.B., D.S.O., M.C., *General Officer, Commanding-in-Chief, Southeastern Command*

General Sir John Davidson, *Colonel, Commandant of Sixtieth Rifles of King's Royal Rifle Corps*

Colonel Mallinson, *Home Guard Zone Commander*

General Franklin, *Home Guard Zone Commander*

Colonel Ebenezer Pike, *Home Guard Zone Commander*

Major Krabbe, *Home Guard Battalion Commander*

General R. Manley-Sims, *Home Guard Nodal Commander*

Colonel Paris, *Home Guard Commander (Air Plane Factory)*

General Sir George MacMunn, *Home Guard Commander*

Colonel Eric Smith, *Home Guard Commander*

Colonel Shelmerdine, *Home Guard Commander*

Colonel Rothband, *Home Guard Commander*

Captain E. H. Ryley, *Deputy Assistant Director, Home Guard Directorate, War Office*

Major Dalby, G.S.O., *War Office (M.T.7)*

Ambassador Winant, *American Embassy*

Mr. Benjamin Cohen, *Legal Adviser to the Ambassador*

General Michael Scanlon, *Air Attaché, American Embassy*

Other Officers Military, Marine and Air Forces at American Embassy

Major E. W. Ridings, *U. S. Army, Head of Civil Defence Committee, sent by War Department of Washington to Study the A.R.P.*

Lt. Colonel Wouters, *Belgian Military Attaché*

Captain Schoonenberg, *Dutch Military Mission*

Major Peterson, *Norwegian Military Mission*

General Fleischer, *Norwegian Military Mission, Commander-in-Chief Norwegian Forces*

Mr. Trygve Lie, *Norwegian Minister of Foreign Affairs*

Captain T. Torkz, *General Staff Polish Army*

Major Sephan Dobsowolski, *Polish Military Mission*

This list does not include the names of many English and American officers, Home Guard Commanders, non-commissioned officers of the Home Guard, and men down the line who furnished us with much valuable information.

PART ONE—INTRODUCTION

Section A. Occasion

Comment by Sir Edward Grigg

SECTION A—*Occasion.*

"When the world was darkened by the eclipse of France, one fact stood out, and that was the extent to which mechanized raiding parties had terrorized whole country-sides, destroyed communication and dislocated the national life. The result in a matter of days was universal confusion crippling both the will and the power to resist. The horror of that spectacle stirred this country to its depths. At that time men of all ages in all parts of the country were eating their hearts out because for one reason or another they had no opportunity of offering military service of one kind or another. Some were too old; others were debarred by their occupations from joining the fighting services. Therefore, the demand for some opportunity of service was intense. From end to end of the country men swore that what happened in France should not happen here. That was the origin of the Home Guard."

The above was a contemporary statement made in reference to the formation of the Home Guard by Sir Edward Grigg, the Joint Under-Secretary of State for War, before the House of Commons.

Section B. Recent History Indicating Military Necessity of Such a Force as the British Home Guard

Comment by Gen. Sir Alan Brooke

SECTION B—*Recent History Indicating Military Necessity of such a Force as the British Home Guard.*

On March 20, 1941 we had an interview with General Sir Alan Brooke, Commander-in-Chief of all the Forces in the British Isles. This interview covered many points. The following is a summary of part of what he said,—

"The Germans have developed a strategy of infiltration which results in the battlefields not being confined to front lines of the opposing forces. To meet this strategy and its accompanying tactics, there must be a widely dispersed force to take the shock of the enemy's primary attacks. Consequently, the most modern defensive strategy involves just such a force as the Home Guard and its function is just as important to the organization of the defence of a country as the functions of any of the other forces such as the regular army."

What were the events which led the British General Staff to the conclusion as above stated by General Sir Alan Brooke? In the balance of this Section of the report are set out the results of our investigation. We interviewed many British Officers who had been through the disastrous events of 1940 leading up to Dunkirk. In addition we talked with Polish, Norwegian, Dutch, Belgian and French officers who had fought through the German campaigns against their countries. Lastly we studied under the former Chief of Operations, International Brigade Staff, and the former Commander of the British Battalion, International Brigade, Spanish Republican Army, now instructors at War Office School No. 1. These men fought against the modern German and Italian mechanized material in Spain.

Spain

1. SPAIN—*(Wintringham and Slater).*

Both Germany and Italy used the Spanish Civil War as a proving ground for their new war material and their tactics of infiltration. The Spanish Republican Forces had some Russian material of the same type. The experience in Spain proved that the defense must be organized in great depth by means of posts and strong points, not the continous lines of the first World War. It also proved that comparatively small groups of determined men using field fortifications and villages or cities could with the ordinary arms stop the modern equipment. In this Civil War the Republican forces developed effectively the use of hand bombs against tanks.

Poland

2. POLAND—*(Major Dowbrowolski and Colonel Tokrz)*

Fifth Column activities and landing of parachute troops without opposition, which completely disrupted lines of communication and disorganized the rear of the Polish Armies "Would have been minimized by the existence of some such local force as the British Home Guard."

Norway

3. NORWAY—*(Mr. Trygve Lie, General Fleischer and Major Peterson)*

By the surprise of its initial attack on Norway, Germany was able by the employment of very few troops to obtain an advantage that the Norwegians and British acting with them were never able to overcome. They seized all the aerodromes in southern and central Norway, every port where heavy military material, such as guns, trucks and armoured cars could be landed, the termini of the Oslo-Trondheim, Oslo-Bergen and Oslo-Kristiansand highroads and railways, the chief cities and most of the magazines and depots of the Norwegian Army. They seized the control of the communications system of the country, including the telegraph, telephone and radio. This situation created such confusion throughout the country that the Norwegian effort was paralyzed. All of this resulted from the effort of very small numbers of German troops who could have been met successfully, particularly in the initial stages, by such an organization as the British Home Guard.

Holland

4. HOLLAND—*(Captain Schoonenberg)*

The German campaign in the Netherlands was characterized by extensive Fifth Column activities combined with such an extensive use of parachute troops and air-borne forces as had never before been witnessed in warfare. The Germans were able to accomplish certain very definite military missions through the employment of these methods. In the first place they were able to seize and hold certain strategically important points such as the Moerdyke Bridge, the Waalhaven Aerodrome at Rotterdam, etc. In the second place they were able to create all over Holland, in the rear of the front line, so many small engagements that they prevented the Dutch reserve troops from being used as previously planned. Most of the Fifth Columnists, parachute troops and air-borne detachments were ultimately wiped out by the Dutch, but the effort of one whole army corps in accomplishing this was such that it was exhausted, dispersed and could not be used as planned. Properly organized and equipped local military units such as the British Home Guard would have prevented the Germans from accomplishing both of the above results.

Belgium and France

5. BELGIUM AND FRANCE—*(Lt. Gen. Eastwood, Gen. Viscount Robert Bridgeman, Colonel Shortt, Lt. Col. Elias-Morgan, Lt. Col. Wouters, Captain Ducq, a French Officer of the Division Legere Motorise (D.L.M.) whose name is not given because his family are still in occupied France).*

The panzer divisions, after the break through, proceeded at will and without resistance through the countryside in the rear of the armies, creating a confusion and disorganization which contributed largely to the ultimate German success. The civilian population fled in great disorder and blocked the roads so that the defending armies were tremendously handicapped.

Such a local force as the Home Guard completely covering the rear areas would have served to eliminate these two factors which contributed greatly to the success of the German Blitz.

Force Similar to Home Guard Force Necessary

An analysis of the German Blitz tactics has led the High Commands of the British and also those of the invaded countries to come to two conclusions; that the only way to meet the German offensive tactics of penetrating the defense with their panzer divisions and air-forces, is by the use of like forces in the counter-offense, and second, the corollary that to give the counter-offense opportunity to go into action effectively, a complementary strategically static, local defense force should be organized. In order not to disrupt production this force must be raised locally from the producers of the country volunteering part of their free time for this service. A local force, through the use of its peculiar knowledge of the terrain, if properly instructed in the use of that terrain for defense, can be effective against the most modern German equipment. A force organized in a similar way to that of the British Home Guard is, therefore, indicated as a strategic necessity in modern warfare. The tactics which naturally follow from its particular function will be outlined in Part Two of this Summary Report.

OFFICIAL OPINION OF THE IMPORTANCE OF THE HOME GUARD

Official Opinion on the Importance of the Home Guard

Mr. Winston Churchill, Prime Minister

stated that "the Home Guard is as much a part of the Army as the Grenadier Guards," and in his speech before the House of Commons on November 5th, 1940, Mr. Churchill said,—"A country where every street and every village bristles with loyal, resolute armed men is a country against which the kind of tactics which destroyed Dutch resistance—tactics of parachutists or air-borne troops in carriers or gliders, Fifth Column activities—... would prove wholly ineffective. A country so defended would not be liable to be overthrown by such tactics."

Mr. David Margesson, Secretary of State for War

stated to us that he was not speaking as a member of the High Command, but from the point of view of the Government,— in other words as a Statesman,—"And," he said, "from the point of view of the responsible Government in planning the defense of England, the Home Guard Force plays absolutely a vital and important part in the plans for defense." He expressed as his opinion that a country could not depend upon its regular forces alone to defend it, but must have a large body of local defense troops to cooperate with the regular forces, as well as all the other organizations such as those grouped under the A.R.P. He stated that from the point of view of the statesman, this type of force must be so organized as not to interfere with the productive capacity of the country,—"And this," said he, "we have accomplished in England with the Home Guard." "At first," he said, "it was a question as to how effective such an organization might be." He pointed out, "that the more we know of the facts of last April, May and June, the more convinced we are that even against modern equipment such a force as the Home Guard can be effective." From the point of view of one responsible for the defense of a country, he said,—"With the experience that we now have behind us, all of the defense organizations should be planned and organized from the start so that their establishment does not conflict with each other, so that the defense of the country will be organized as a whole."

We have already quoted at the beginning of this section the opinion of General Sir Alan Brooke.

In our main report we give the opinions of several other men of importance.

Section C. History

Picture before English People May 1940

SECTION C—*History*.

The tragic results of the invasion of Norway, Holland and Belgium and what was happening in France in the month of May 1940 were being impressed upon British people with greater speed and greater force. The Germans had introduced new tactics of warfare. The British people themselves saw this picture and England was day by day being put in a more and more vulnerable position. Referring to this situation Sir Edward Grigg said,—"From end to end of the country men swore that what happened to France should not happen here." He further said, "We are living under conditions where imminent peril may descend upon us from the sky at any moment in the dawn tomorrow or in the dusk tomorrow night—we cannot tell."

Birth of the Home Guard May 14, 1940

It was on the evening of May 14th, 1940 that the Right Honorable Anthony Eden, M.C., the then Secretary of State for War, broadcast an address to the British people. He said in part,—

"I want to speak to you tonight about a form of warfare which the Germans have been employing so extensively against Holland and Belgium . . . . We are going to ask you to help in a manner which I know will be welcome to thousands of you. The Government has received inquires from all over the Kingdom from men who wish to do something for the defense of the country. Now is your opportunity. We want large numbers of such men . . . . between the ages of 17 and 65 to come forward now and offer their services. The name of the new Force will be Local Defense Volunteers. In order to volunteer what you have to do is to give in your name at your local police station . . . . . "

The result of the broadcast was electrifying.

By May 20th, in a period of only six days, 250,000 volunteers had come forward.

By the middle of July in 1940 the Force had reached the figure of 1,300,000 volunteers.

By the middle of November, the Home Guard numbered 1,700,000.

Conception

Statement by Tom Wintringham

Though there has been a very definite evolution in the conception of the function of the Home Guard, the following quotations from Mr. Thomas Wintringham, an ex-officer in the International Brigade in Spain during the Civil War, indicates the thought which led so many patriotic Englishmen to volunteer and also indicates the thought of the War Office which was behind the organization of the Force.

"Many of the Home Guard are ex-service men with real and valuable experience of War to their credit, but since the days when they helped to defeat the greatest military machine in Europe, methods of warfare have changed. War has become more rapid, more complex and given greater opportunities to small units, whose leaders have initiative and intelligence . . . . . the obvious answer to these new tactics of the Germans is provided in Britain by the Home Guard. Because of its organization and its local character the Home Guard is a force that cannot be pierced. It is not a line on the map. It fills the whole map. No attack can get beyond it to an unarmed, unprotected area . . . . . there is no 'beyond' . . . . . it may not hold against strong and concentrated enemy forces. Its business is to delay and weary such forces, aiding our own regulars in their counter-attacks and taking as its special targets the forward units of the enemy forces and the stragglers on the fringe of the main advance ..... part of the Home Guard's job is to carry on the struggle if necessary in areas temporarily overrun by the enemy. This last duty it can carry out if it learns some of the tactics of guerrilla warfare. All its duties make it necessary that the Home Guard should learn how to act as observation and combat patrols. They must learn how to stalk the enemy, as well as learning the art of holding a defence position for as long as possible, forcing the enemy to check his advance, and to deploy all his forces before his opponents slip away from his grip. Another character of modern German tactics that must be noted by the Home Guard is their extreme ruthlessness, and of course our training is intended to give the Home Guard confidence that they can kill Germans with the weapons with which they are armed, or with which they can improvise, and that it is right and proper to do so."

German Reaction

The immediate reaction of the German authorities to the news of the formation of such a force was to announce that in the event of its members being captured by them with arms in their hands, they would be treated as "Franc-tireurs" and shot. Dr. Goebbels at first referred to the L.D.V. as a "rabble" and a "mob of amateurs armed with broom-sticks and darts," but it was not long after that, however, before he was obliged to revise his comments. He was able, apparently, to find out that this was not a group of "amateurs," that it was not armed with "broom-sticks and darts" but that it was a very vital force, playing an important part in the defence of its country. It was then that Dr. Goebbels referred to the L.D.V. as "gangsters and murders—franc-tireurs."

Status

The facts are that the Home Guard is a part of the Crown Forces in England. They are uniformed, they carry arms openly, are properly officered, and they have the same standing and rights at international law as any full-time soldier of the regular field forces.

Early Sporadic Movements of Local Defence

Even before the government took any action for the formation of the L.D.V. various small groups and private individuals were not only talking but were organizing for defence in their own localities. As General Lord Robert Bridgeman pointed out to us this was unfortunate because, after one basic plan under the control of the War Office was decided upon, it made it more difficult to undo these sporadic movements and fit them into the whole.

History of Organization

Part Three, Section H of this Summary Report deals with present organization, etc., but some comments properly belong here in this sketch of the History. When Mr. Anthony Eden made his radio appeal to the people of England on May 14, 1940, asking volunteers to register with the police, no steps had been taken to legalize the force, that is, provide properly for its existence. This was done by an Order in Council three days later, on May 17th, and by this Order in Council the establishment and control of the new force was made the responsibility of the Army Council. One can picture the confusion resulting from the registration of thousands of volunteers when no one had any instructions as to how the force was to be organized. The Army Council immediately put the force under the commander of all the regular forces in the British Isles and passed the job of organizing the force over to the regular commanders of the military areas into which England was divided, providing that in each military area a Home Guard area organizer should be appointed. These were to be chosen with the help of the Lord Lieutenants of the counties. In turn these area organizers appointed Zone commanders, and Zone commanders appointed Group commanders, Battalion commanders, etc. It was the section commanders who organized their own particular sections in their small localities. This was all done in a most informal way without any official regulations until, on June 24th, the Army Council issued A.C.I. No. 653.

Responsibility in Army Council

Help from Police

The old and well established Police Force with its intimate knowledge of the people of each locality contributed largely in their recommendations and the checking of individual applicants.

Inspector General of L.D.V.

The Army Council which is responsible for the entire conduct of the British war effort attempted shortly to delegate some of its responsibility for the Home Guard. When General Pownell, who had been Lord Gort's Chief-of-Staff, returned from France he was appointed Inspector General of the L.D.Vs. This position did not, however, carry with it the right to issue orders. The authority still rested with the Army Council and consequently orders had to be issued from the War Office. General Pownell, having determined what he thought should be done had to put his orders through the War Office, which caused great delay and some confusion. This ultimately led to the appointment of a Director General for the Home Guard with a proper Directorate in the War Office. To him was delegated the Army Council's authority, so that he could issue orders in its name. In the meanwhile the Army Council issued some training instructions. The first one was gotten out in May and dealt with the subject of road blocks and defense of villages. These instructions which followed from time to time were used by the local commanders as a basis for training their Home Guard units.

Appointment of Home Guard Directorate

Osterly Park School for Home Guard Instruction

In June Mr. Thomas Wintringham, who was eminently fitted to instruct the Home Guard because of his experience in Spain, formed the Osterly Park School under the sponsorship of Mr. Edward Houlton of the Picture Post. The School was actually opened on July 10, 1940. The course at first was only a two days' course, the object being to teach some of the Home Guard commanders and non-commissioned officers the use of such arms as were available or could be improvised against enemy invasion as had been learned in Spain. Osterly even attracted some of the officers of the Regular Army and finally, in September after having graduated 5000 members the school was fully recognized and taken over by the War Office as War Office School No. 1. The course today has been extended to six days.

Gen. Eastwood as Director General of Home Guard

It was in November that it was decided that for the proper handling of the Home Guard it should be given its own Directorate in the War Office. It is to be noted that they picked as Director General one of the foremost young generals in the British Army, General Eastwood, who had been General Sir Alan Brooke's Chief-of-Staff in France. When Lord Gort was recalled to England, General Sir Alan Brooke had been given command temporarily of what was left of the B.E.F. and was put in command of all the British Forces in the British Isles after the continent was abandoned. It was his former Chief-of-Staff who was picked as Director General of the Home Guard. This Directorate has general charge of coordinating all of the activities of the Home Guard. It is the direct contact between the officers of the Home Guard in the field and the Army Council. The chain of operational command passes into the regular army chain of command in the military areas, but all the administrative work heads up into the Directorate.

Territorial Associations

When the War Office was suddenly faced, in May of 1940, with the administration of a large and rapidly growing force, the new L.D.Vs., it seized upon the already existent Territorial Army Associations as instruments through which to administer it. The Territorial Army was a force rather similar to our National Guard in the United States. In England there were, of course, no such local sub-divisions as states so that the general plan of the Territorial Army was based on County Regiments. Each County Regiment had its Association which looked after the continuing interests of the Regiment. Prominent men in the county and ex-officers of the Regiment were very active in these organizations. The Territorial Army Directorate in the War Office worked through them and coordinated the responsibilities of the different members of the Army Council and the different departments of the War Office in relation to the organization and administration of the Territorial Army. With the outbreak of the War in 1939, the Territorial Army was absorbed into the regular Crown Forces so that there was ready made and at hand, at the time of the organization of the L.D.Vs., a group of associations which could be used for most of the administrative work of the new force.

Early Work

As stated above, it was in May 1940 that the War Office under the authority of the Chief of the Imperial General Staff, a member of the Army Council issued its first instruction, designated Training Instruction No. 1, 1940. This instruction dealt with the subject of road blocks and defense of villages. Although today it is the responsibility of the regular field forces to plan for and design the type of defenses required for any particular position, nevertheless, owing to the emergency at the times, the L.D.Vs. set feverishly to work to build the defenses of their localities. In many instances the job of designing and building the defenses was turned over to willing but inefficient hands with the result that many defense stations were poorly sited and constructed, not making a proper use of camouflage and not taking proper advantage of the protection that nature itself offered. Many such sites were very conspicuous, so much so that a lot of the work had to be done over.

Army Council Instructions

As stated above, it was on June 24, 1940, that the Army Council issued its first important "Instruction" concerning the L.D.V., No. 653, 1940. This was the first general basic instruction issued to the L.D.Vs., but as new problems were constantly presenting themselves there was issued on August 15, 1940 Army Council Instruction No. 924, which covered in greater breadth and detail the matters originally mentioned in A.C.I. No. 653. In fact this new A.C.I. No. 924 still remained on April 1, 1941 the basis for the Home Guard organization and administration.

Name of the Force Changed from L.D.V. to Home Guard July 1940

In the meanwhile the name of this Force was changed from Local Defence Volunteers to the Home Guard. We were informed that this was at the instigation of Mr. Winston Churchill who felt that the name Home Guard more correctly described the part that the Volunteers were to play in the general scheme of total defense. In fact in his broadcast on July 14, 1940, Mr. Churchill had this to say,—". . . The Local Defence Volunteers, or as they might better be called the Home Guard . . . ".

As the requirements of the Home Guard became more apparent, as new problems arose, and as unthought-of contingencies developed, there were issued from time to time from the War Office "Home Guard Training Instructions" and "Army Council Instructions," all of which are covered in detail in our main report, as well as being referred to in various sections of this summary report.

Home Guard a Force of 1,750,000

Since its birth a year ago the Home Guard has grown lustily. It now aggregates about 1,750,000 volunteers. It reaches into every great city, including London, every town, village and hamlet. The large cities are organized into defensive zones and sectors. The towns are less elaborately organized. Practically every village in the land is planned as a strong point. It is to be remembered that most of these villages control important highways. Every important group of factories is organized into a defensive zone. Many large individual factories have their own special plan of defense. The railways and other public utilities are similarly defended. The outlying posts and patrols of the Home Guard reach out into the uninhabited districts such as downs and moors. The Regular Army has given its attention to the defensive plans of all the Home Guard Units and those plans are tied closely to and coordinated with those of the regular field forces.

Many of the original organizers have been eliminated and today the Force is properly led by Home Guard Commanders to whom King's Commissions have been issued.

As stated above, this Force is accepted by the British High Command as a part of the Regular Crown Forces with a very definite function in the plans for the defense of England.

Spirit and Morale

To complete a picture of the development of the Home Guard, three natural queries should be answered.
1. Who were the volunteers who rallied to the defense of their country and created this Force?
2. What is the spirit and morale of this Force? (This question is closely coupled to the first.)
3. What effect did the emergence of this Force have on the Country as a whole?

All Classes Volunteer for Home Guard

Immediately following Mr. Anthony Eden's broadcast in May 1940, people of all classes and conditions from 17 years of age to 65 offered their services to the country.

Comment by Gen. Eastwood

Lt. General T. R. Eastwood, Director General of the Home Guards, in a very concise way summed up for us the friendliness and the spirit of cooperation of the individuals who have volunteered for the Home Guard Force—

"There has been an extraordinary getting together of all classes creating a sympathetic understanding of how the other fellow lives and the realization of the good there is in each other regardless of class. A Colonel or an Admiral of the old days and now in the ranks of the Home Guards as a private soldier, may be rubbing shoulders with a man who drives a butcher cart, a clerk, a worker in a factory, a farmer, a business man, or a lawyer."

Ex-High Ranking Officers Now Soldiers in Home Guard

Retired Generals and retired officers of high rank have enlisted as private soldiers or have taken commands of low rank, accepting those positions as a matter of course. Lt. General Fisher, who was commanding the Southern Army Command until after Dunkirk, and now retired from the Regular Forces on account of age, is today Lance Corporal in the Home Guard, having just been promoted from the ranks. In one of the Zones the Company Commanders are as follows—

Two Retired Brigadier Generals

One Retired Adjutant General

One man who has never been in the army before

An officer attached to the American Embassy in England told us of dining with an old gentleman, Lord X., at his home just outside of London. After dinner Lord X. asked the officer if he would like to take a little walk around the grounds—whereupon the butler, who was a commander in the Home Guard, stepped up to Lord X. and said— "Pardon me, your Lordship, but you will have to wait a few minutes until I give permission to the Home Guard Patrol to allow you to pass through the grounds." (The grounds of Lord X. had been specified as a vulnerable spot and were under patrol by the Home Guard.)

Our main report deals with many other interesting and notable instances.

It has been officially estimated that forty percent of the Home Guard Force is made up of ex-service men.

Everybody a Worker

Almost everyone in this force is a worker, carrying on during the day their civilian jobs. After their day's work is done, (and it is a long day, too), they give up two and perhaps three evenings a week to Home Guard duties. On Saturday afternoons and Sundays, although their normal time for fun and recreation, these Home Guard men go out for drill or manoeuvres, or the building of road blocks, or the repairing of pill-boxes, or digging trenches. As one old ex-sergeant said to us,— "These birds never watch the clock. They are never ready to quit."

Comments by J. K. H. and H. W. E.

It was obvious to us in our inspection of the various Home Guard Units that the unselfish offering of all classes of the British to the service of their country, had created within this Force an unique spirit. The methods of "Colonel Blimp" had disappeared. The officers were proud of their men—were patient—cooperative—and understanding. The men themselves were keen on their job—were proud of the part they were playing—facing the future with courage and determination. Many times when we were inspecting them in their action stations, have the men whispered to us that they were "just itching to pull the trigger on the Bosche." We have seen them carrying out their practice manoeuvres at night while their city was undergoing an air raid, German planes overhead, the crash and smash of anti-aircraft guns and shells bursting in air, and yet these men kept quietly on with their job.

Effect of Home Guard on Morale of Population

Not only did the surging up of the British people to form this Force have a direct effect on the volunteers themselves, but indirectly the formation of the Home Guard had a very definite effect on the population-at-large. We believe that the comments made to us by General Eastwood give a very comprehensive summary,—"There has developed a fundamental change. For the first time, as never before, a greater and greater trust has been placed in the population. The Government is trusting its people with the care of the Crown's arms." "Could you," he said, "ever imagine a dictator's state ever trusting its people in that way?"

Comments by Gen. Eastwood

Continuing on this subject of morale, he said,—"Following the evacuation at Dunkirk the whole country was aroused at the seriousness of the situation. With the development of the Home Guard the tempo of apprehension of the civil population changed. The father of the family, or the son, while keeping on with his job joined the Home Guard. On certain nights during the week and on Saturdays or Sundays he gave up his time for training or preparing defense positions. At other times he was at home discussing with his family, his work for and ideas about the defense of his country. His wife, or his daughter, or his sister, became a part of the defense, either actively or in spirit. They knew that father or brother was actually with gun or grenade defending their own home and themselves. They knew that Mr. X. and Mr. Y. and Mr. Z. with other neighbors or workers were defending their factories and their plants. And so today our people face the future with assurance and courage. The development of the Home Guard has done just that."

We have discussed this psychological effect at length with many other men of importance. In fact, Sir Edward Grigg, Joint Under-Secretary of State for War, stated to us that the courage and fortitude of the people had been brought about largely by the Home Guard.

We will in our main report record numerous important comments from men of high standing. We note, however, in this Summary Report a few of them, as follows—

Comment by Lt. Col. Sir Thomas Moore, M.P.

Lt. Col. Sir Thomas Moore, M.P., stated—". . . and this (The Home Guard) is one of the most important movements which has taken place in this country."

Comment by Col. Ebenezer Pike

Colonel Ebenezer Pike, a Zone Commander, said this to us—"The Home Guard has been the means of maintaining an excellent citizen morale."

It is interesting to note here that Colonel Pike introduced the novelty of bringing the wives of the Home Guard volunteers into many of the evening lectures with the result that it created in the families themselves a feeling of confidence and a feeling that they were a part of the scheme of defense. Such families will not be the willing or innocent tools of Fifth Column Agents. They understand fully the dangers of ignorant and uncontrolled panic.

It is the opinion of many people in England that the formation of the Home Guard had a direct effect upon the Germans' intention to invade England.

Comment by General Sir Cecil Romer

General Sir Cecil Romer, who acts in a special capacity as Adviser to the Home Guard, made this observation to us,—"The very formation and organization of the Home Guard have had a lot to do in stopping or delaying Hitler from invading England."

Comment by Mr. Lawson, M.P.

Mr. Lawson, M.P., said before the House of Commons on November 15, 1940—"But a few months ago we dared scarcely breathe for the danger of the British invasion.... The Home Guard by its emergence played no little part in standing off those who would invade this country.... It is a fact that the determination of the British people expressed through the Home Guard had a profound effect upon our enemy and played a great part in standing off invasion."

Comment by Major Lord Denham

Major Lord Denham, Liaison Officer, expressed his opinion to us as follows—"Unquestionably the formation of the Home Guard has had a tremendous effect in warding off or delaying at least, an invasion of England."

From the point of view of the United States it may be well to remember that though such a force may never be needed in this country to defend us against invasion, its very existence may be a factor in the mind of any enemy who is considering such an invasion.

PART TWO—TACTICS AND TRAINING.

Section D. Tactics

The tactical employment of the Home Guard naturally follows from the strategical function of the force.

Early Conception

During the year of its existence the conception of the tactical employment of the Home Guard has changed. At first it was conceived largely as a force to meet parachute troops and its members were colloquially known as the "Parashots." This was because of the tremendous reaction to the use by the Germans in Holland of parachute and air-borne troops. Then, as information of the German campaigns in Flanders and France began to leak back to England it became apparent that there were other jobs for such a local defense force as the Home Guard. Less emphasis was put on its anti-parachute duties. The first conception was of sprinkling the whole land with small detachments for the purposes of detecting the presence of and delaying the motor-cycle, light armoured-car and tank detachments of the Germans in the event of invasion, as well as their parachute and air-borne troops.

Defense of Strong Points

As more information came from the Continent and was analyzed, it was realized that to make such a force effective it should be used to organize really strong defensive points throughout the land. Consequently the present conception of the use of the force has resulted in drawing the scattered units into greater density at appropriate positions, positions which lend themselves naturally to organization for defense against the German equipment and tactics and as centers from which to carry on guerrilla warfare.

The Three Tactical Functions

The tactical functions of the Home Guard can for general purposes be grouped into three large categories:
1. Warning.
2. Delaying.
3. Harassing.

These are the three types of action which can be successfully carried out by forces armed in the manner which necessarily will be the lot of such an organization.

The available arms necessarily have a direct effect on the tactics to be employed. Two units, differently armed, may accomplish the same mission by employing different tactics. The arms of the Home Guard have consequently had a direct effect on that force's tactical plans. In Great Britain there has been a very definite limitation upon the arms of the Home Guard, through necessity. This has been progressively changing over the history of the force, and the Home Guard is being better and better armed. Aside from the necessities of the situation in England the fact that this force must, for economic reasons, be composed of part-time soldiers and that they must not be taken far from their work or homes does, however, have a limiting effect on the arms with which the force can or should be armed, and consequently it would seem to be true that the arms of any such force wherever organized, and, if there were no limitations from necessity, would have an effect upon its tactical employment. (For the arms of the Home Guard see p. 25.)

Warning

Warning:

The Home Guard through patrols, outlying posts and ordinary observation posts can keep a fairly thorough and continuous observation over the whole of a threatened area. In the British Isles this is the whole country.

Delaying

Delaying:

In the case of parachute troops or air-borne landings, including crash landings, the mission of the Home Guard is first to warn the regular forces, and second, to get to the spot as soon as possible, attempt, if they can, to wipe out the enemy, but, if the enemy has landed in too great force, their mission is to surround and contain it, keeping the enemy from spreading and always knowing where it is.

Delaying (Defensive Positions)

In the case of successful invasion by land forces the mission of the Home Guard is to delay the fast moving mechanized detachments and columns of the enemy, prevent them from running wild, from destroying all communications, and from creating complete confusion. This they do by firing on and holding up the advanced scouting units of the enemy and by falling back upon and manning their prepared defensive positions. These defensive positions are organized into strong points. Such strong points are organized about important road junctions, bridges, tunnels, etc., or even within a town. Any place on important roads where nature gives a good opportunity for field fortification may also be organized into a strong point to deny the use of the road to the enemy. In the organization of these strong points, trenches (particularly narrow slit trenches), road blocks, pill boxes, and other field fortifications are prepared. All brick and stone construction, such as houses within a village, have proved to be effective defenses against tanks and armoured cars, consequently the Home Guard take advantage of all such objects in the organization of their strong points.

Delaying (Nodal Points)

Certain positions are of such great importance that they are designated as "Nodal Points" and here the mission of the Home Guard is to hold the position as long as possible. They are supposed to die fighting, without surrendering the position to the enemy. A village or town that controls an important main road, railway, electric or water supply, etc., would be an example of such a nodal point.

Factories

All important groups of factories, or single factories, if from a tactical point of view it is preferable, are organized into defensive units. The Home Guards for the defense of such units are drawn from the factory workers themselves.

Towns and Cities

Towns and cities, even to the largest, London itself, are organized as defense zones. The defense of a large city involves the blocking of all the bridges, roads and railways into the city. It may involve quite extensive tank barriers, such as surrounding anti-tank ditches, with the appropriate road blocks where roads cross the line. The organization of the city may involve the planning of several concentric lines of defense within the city, around a keep. It involves the construction of well-camouflaged posts within the houses and along the main arteries. It involves the use of subways, sewer systems, etc., for intercommunication.

Though the Home Guard is strategically static, each unit for the purpose of defending its own locality is tactically mobile within its locality.

Delaying ("Scorched Earth" Mission)

Another group of jobs assigned to the Home Guard can be characterized as its "scorched earth" mission. We did not hear this characterization in England, but we are familiar with the term as it has been used to express the Chinese policy. Falling within this mission is the Home Guard's responsibility for immobilizing transportation facilities including not only automobiles, trucks, etc., but also the fuel supply such as gasoline and oil. Another responsibility is the destruction or removal of all food and water supply which might fall into the hands of the enemy. Another responsibility is the control of the civilian population, denying its use as a screen to the enemy and preventing its panicky movements from congesting the roads and hindering military operations.

Duty as Guides

In connection with one of the duties of the Home Guard it is to be remembered that there are no sign posts or even private signs indicating geographical locality. It is surprising how difficult it is to move about in a country that has no such normal helps. The Home Guard is responsible for the enforcing of this handicap to the enemy, and in turn providing guides for British troops.

Harassing

Harassing:

One of the missions of the Home Guard is to harass the enemy. To this end they are taught the niceties of guerrilla warfare.

The manning of tanks and their operation is very tiring and difficult on the crews. The Home Guard is particularly trained to watch for enemy tanks, never giving them a moment's rest or chance to open up their armor so as to get more air, to keep them in a continual state of nerves through the use of booby traps, mines, etc. The same thing is true of all the enemy forces. Once the enemy is in the country, it is the duty of the Home Guard to see that they have no rest at night without being threatened with raiding, etc., and in the daytime to harass the enemy with sniping. Another duty of the Home Guard is to continually raid the supply lines. The object of all this is to give the enemy no chance to rest and relax and to keep them, if possible, in a continual state of jitters. The local character of the Home Guard is a great asset in fulfilling this mission. They know every back alley, every highway and byway, every short-cut and ditch. They know all the hills, valleys and hollows. They know the woodlands and how to get through them.

Special Arms and Methods

Because of the peculiar tactical function of the Home Guard, in addition to the usual small arms, certain special arms have been invented or developed to enable it to accomplish that function. Grenades or bombs for use against tanks have been developed and projectors to throw them. In addition there have been certain developments of flame-throwing apparatus and the use of oil against tanks such as the Fougasse and "Hedge-hopper." All of this will be dealt with in greater detail in the study of training.

Section E. Training
Organization

SECTION E—*Training.*
Organization:

The Defense (Local Defense Volunteers) Regulations, 1940 places the responsibility for the training of the Home Guard on the Army Council. The Army Council fulfils its duties in relation to the training of the Home Guard through the Director of Military Training and his Directorate in the War Office. There is a special branch of this Directorate known as M.T.7, which has full charge of the training of the Home Guard. There is one exception to this; the training of those units of the Home Guard which are specially allotted to anti-aircraft duties comes under the Director of Anti-Aircraft and Coast Defense and his Directorate in the War Office. In describing here the general set-up for the training of the Home Guard this exception will not be included.

Director Military Training

Staff Officers

Each Army Command Headquarters and each Military Area Headquarters have attached to them a General Staff Officer (regular army) one of whose responsibilities is the training of the Home Guard. Particularly is this officer of the area responsible for the organization and general supervision of the training of the Home Guard in his area. He sees that the Home Guard units are affiliated to some regular army formation for training purposes and he is the channel to and from M.T.7.

General Training— Unit Commanders

As in all military organizations the bulk of the training of the troops falls to the lot of the unit commanders. These unit commanders pick from their commands men particularly fitted for instructing in various subjects and for organizing schools within their units—company, battalion, etc. As will appear later these instructors are given special opportunities to prepare themselves for their work. In addition to these instructors drawn from the units themselves, the regular army furnishes instructors from those regular army units most closely associated with the Home Guard Units involved. These regular army instructors act in two ways. Sometimes they instruct the Home Guard Unit as a whole, more often they teach the instructors of the unit.

Regular Army Cooperation

Selected men from the Home Guard are also permitted to attend the unit schools of Company and Battalion, of the Regular Army Units.

Permanent Staff Instructors

In addition to these regular army instructors furnished by adjacent regular army units, certain experienced men are enlisted as Warrant Officers or Sergeants in the regular army and are posted as Permanent Staff Instructors to the Home Guard. A pool of these Permanent Staff Instructors is maintained at each Army Command Headquarters. This pool circulates among the units of the Home Guard falling within the command. In addition one Permanent Staff Instructor is posted to each Home Guard Battalion and each unit guarding a large Public Utility Company, such as a Railroad. It would be difficult for these instructors to reach areas in which small Home Guard Units are scattered, consequently there is a special Permanent Staff Instructor for about every six Battalions to take care of this situation. All of these Permanent Staff Instructors are given the opportunity of taking courses at the Army Command Regular Schools, such as Weapon Schools, etc.

Area and Sub-Area Schools

In addition, the P.S.Is. of the Army Command Pool organize schools in the Areas or Sub-Areas of the Command. The Home Guard Unit Instructors attend these schools.

War Office Schools

In addition to this M.T.7. has established two special schools for Home Guard Officers and N.C.O.s who return to their units as instructors. Number One is in England and Number Two is in Scotland. A very recent development is the establishment of a Traveling Wing of War Office School No. 1. Colloquially this Traveling School is referred to as a "Circus." Its purpose is to conduct weekend courses in the more isolated country districts and in the larger centers of population for those instructors of the Home Guard who can not attend one of the regular schools. The two regular schools give a week's concentrated course in the tactical functions of the Home Guard and in the application of its arms to those functions. We had the privilege of taking the course at War Office School No. 1.

Training Publications

The War Office through M.T.7. issues "Home Guard Instructions." By April 1st, 1941 26 of these Instructions had been issued. They cover in a minor way the role or mission of the Home Guard, its organization, and more particularly its training. In addition, M.T.7. issues to the Home Guard some of the pamphlets, manuals, field service pocketbooks, etc., prepared for the regular forces. These publications will be referred to in the paragraphs below on training in specific subjects.

Our main report, in preparation, will include all of these official publications, as exhibits.

General

The routine operations of the Home Guard of course include not only their training but their non-combatant duties which they constantly perform, such as anti-sabotage, anti-espionage and observation. They are all constantly on watch for possible fifth columnists. They take their turn at sentry duty and guard duty, as observers in their outlying posts. If their local plan includes patrols, those patrols are out every night. In addition to these duties, they are constantly training for their combatant mission in case of invasion. During the first months of their organization, they were busy preparing their defense positions; digging trenches, building road blocks, pill boxes, etc. At the same time they were doing a certain amount of elementary drill and learning something about their arms as they received them. As winter approached and the danger of invasion became less, the opportunity was taken to ground the men more thoroughly in the care and use of their arms. As greater proficiency was obtained in this essential, more and more emphasis in the training was placed on lectures and tactical exercises to perfect them in fulfilling their particular roles in their own locality. We will now describe in more detail some of the above training.

Drill

Drill: The attitude in the British Home Guards towards drill was well expressed by Mr. George Orwell in an article on the Home Guard in the Evening Standard of January 8, 1941, "a part-time force cannot emulate the regulars in parade-ground smartness and ought not to try, since it needs all the time it can get for the more important arts of shooting, bomb throwing, map reading, distance-judging, taking cover, and the building of tank-traps and fortifications." It is to be noted that in the first four Instructions issued by the War Office, there was no mention of drill. It was not until about the first of August, about three months after the formation of the force, that the War Office gave any instructions as to drill for the Home Guard. This was in Instruction No. 5 where it sets out a few of the simplest movements under the heading "The necessary drill" and ends up by saying "if a unit can do this, it can move organized." The amount of drill actually given in the training varies greatly with the different units. But on the whole, it is kept down to a minimum with the idea that its useful purpose is to enable the Commanders to move their units about in an orderly fashion. Instruction No. 14, which is the directive for the Winter Training (1940-41) sets in Appendix A "certain standards of training to be arrived at." Under "Drill" only the simplest positions and movements are included. It is surprising how "snappily" most of the units go through the simple formations to which their training has been limited. The official Home Guard drill manual was not issued until the end of September, 1940, as Instruction No. 13. It includes only the simplest movements, omitting entirely all parades and ceremonies. The above is true of drill with arms and the manual of arms.

Guard Duty

Guard Duty: Home Guard Instructions Nos. 4, 5, 14 and 19 deal with the subject. Nos. 5 and 19 lay down the procedure for challenging both when active operations are and are not in progress, with particular directions for sentries on roads. These latter are informal and follow in no way the ordinary formalities of Guard Duty. Home Guard Instruction No. 14, which is the directive for the 1940-41 Winter Training sets up in Appendix A, standards to be met in various subjects, but omits any standard for Guard Duty as such.

No official manuals on this subject prepared for the Home Guard have as yet been issued by the War Office, but there are various unofficial manuals which are more or less recognized and used by the Guard itself (several of which will be included in our Main Report as exhibits). A quotation from one of these "A Home Guard Drill Book and Field Service Manual" by John Brophy, Page 101, will perhaps indicate better than any other way the attitude of the Home Guard towards guard duty.

"Sentry Duties.—Except on vulnerable points in cities and heavily populated areas, the Home Guard will not be required to maintain guards with the formality and detail of the regular army. The sentry, not having to march a beat, is usually free to sling his rifle and to maintain some informality of bearing. In country districts, and always in active service conditions, formality and regularity should be dispensed with altogether, apart from the procedure for challenging (when the order is given) anyone approaching. The place to be guarded should thus be thought of as an Observation Post as well as a defence centre."

Very occasionally, more as an honor than otherwise, for instance when the Home Guard had been invited to accept sentry duty at Buckingham Palace, is ceremonial guard mounting undertaken. Formal guard mounting is not included in Home Guard Training. The relief of sentries is carried out in a simple but orderly manner. The Home Guard training is conducted along the line of standing patrols, observation posts and reconnoitering patrols. Great emphasis in the training of the Home Guard is placed on proper observation and reporting of information.

Observation and Reporting of Information

Observation and Reporting of Information: As stated above great emphasis is placed on careful and correct observation and accurate reporting of information in the training of the Home Guard. The number of Home Guard Instructions touching upon this subject is indicative—Nos. 2, 3, 4, 5, 10, 11, 14, 20, 21 and 23. In addition to these Home Guard Instructions there have been issued to the Unit Commanders among others the following Regular Army Instruction pamphlets which deal in part to a greater or less degree with the same subject matter:

Infantry Training—Training and War, 1937; Infantry Section Leading, 1938; Tactical Notes for Platoon Commanders, 1941; Field Service Pocketbook—Orders and Intercommunication, 1939; Field Service Pocketbook—Intelligence—Information and Security, 1939; Pocket Notes on Identification of German Units, 1940; and Notes on Map Reading, 1939.

NOTE: The above "Instructions" and pamphlets will be available as exhibits in our Main Report.

The Home Guard is trained to observe accurately from observation posts and by the use of patrols. In this connection there is much practice in scouting and stalking, searching woods, judging distance and estimating numbers both by sight and sound, keeping unheard and unseen, the latter particularly from the air. Picked men are specially trained as scouts. There are even instructions relative to the use of watch dogs.

Also thorough courses are given in the use of maps and the compass for observation and reporting purposes and the distinguishing between British and German planes and personnel. A great deal of night training is included. Training in the detecting of false rumors, in the preparation of accurate reports—how and what to observe and report. Practice in the sending of messages, including the information to be given and the form to be used, both oral and written; the use of the clock-faced system. These latter matters were first covered in detail in Home Guard Instruction No. 4, which has since been replaced by Home Guard Instruction No. 10. In addition the channels of communication or means of warning are worked out by the Home Guard and practice exercises are carried on. The use of church bells is restricted to the warning of parachute or air-borne landings. The civil, railway, police, and military telephones are employed. The greatest reliance, however, is placed on despatch riders, mounted on bicycles, motorcycles, and in a few cases on horses, also on foot messengers.

Weapon Training

Weapon Training: The weapons of the Home Guard include: the pistol and revolver; the rifle; the automatic rifle (Browning); the Sub-machine-gun (Thompson); the light machine-gun (Browning air-cooled and Lewis air and water cooled); machine-gun—water cooled, 30 caliber (Vickers, originally—Browning); anti-aircraft machine-gun (Vickers, originally—Browning); quick-firing anti-aircraft guns (Hispana); bayonet; grenades and bombs of various kinds; flame throwers, including the Fougasse and "Hedge-hopper"; land mines and booby traps; knives, daggers, etc.

Great emphasis has been placed on the elementary or basic training in all these weapons with the exception of the pistol, the revolver and the bayonet. The training in connection with some of the special grenades or bombs, flame throwers, Fougasse, "hedge-hoppers," land mines and booby traps has naturally been limited to specialists and has for the great number of Home Guard entered more into their tactical exercises than their basic weapon training.

Home Guard Instruction No. 14, the directive for the 1940-41 Winter Training, states "The *main* task in winter training will be for Home Guards to reach an adequate standard in weapon training. This must come first. Each Home Guard must know the weapon or weapons he may have to use."

25

Home Guard Instruction No. 4 places "weapon training" as one of the elements of training for the Home Guard and refers instructors to the group of regular army instruction pamphlets "Small Arms Training Vol. I," always known as "S.A.T." Various of these pamphlets will be referred to below. Home Guard Instruction No. 5 follows this up and states "The standard to be reached is for a man to be certain of a 'kill' if an enemy gives a fair chance at a reasonable distance"—a simple and practical definition of the objective for such a force as the Home Guard.

The Rifle

The Rifle: The first arm for which training instructions were detailed officially was the rifle (Home Guard Instruction No. 5). The subject is also mentioned in Home Guard Instructions Nos. 11, 12, 14, 16, 17, 18 and 26. In addition there have been issued to the Home Guard the following numbered pamphlets of the S.A.T. Vol. I series, which deal with rifle training: 1, 2, 3, 6. The basic training includes the theory of fire; nomenclature and mechanism; stripping and assembling; care and cleaning, including sighting and zeroing; positions—prone, kneeling and standing; marksmanship, including aiming exercises, trigger pressing (squeeze), and range work with sub-caliber rifles (22) on miniature range, work on 30 yard range with service ammunition and on standard range up to 200 yards. Long range practice is reserved for sharp-shooters. Instruction No. 5 states "If a man can shoot at 200 yards so as to kill, this is satisfactory. Efforts should not be wasted at long ranges, nor should a moving target except at very close quarters be fired at. This is waste of effort except for a skilled shot." From conversation with certain Home Guard commanders, we believe that as a practical matter many of the units restrict the range work of the bulk of the members of the Home Guard to 100 yards rather than 200.

Anti-Aircraft Fire

Anti-Aircraft Fire: Although anti-aircraft defense is not normally one of the functions of the Home Guard and, in consequence, Home Guard Units are not normally organized and equipped for that purpose, they must be prepared to use their weapons against low-flying aircraft if they are attacked by them. As mentioned below in Part Three, some Home Guard Units are allotted to anti-aircraft duties. The training of such units conforms to the regular army training for the arms with which they are equipped.

The training in small-arms anti-aircraft fire is the same for the rifle, automatic rifle and light machine-gun. Certain simple instructions were first issued to the Home Guard in Instruction No. 5. It is again touched on in connection with Factory Defense in No. 12. A special Instruction No. 17 was issued dealing solely with anti-aircraft fire which superseded the instructions in No. 5. In addition S.A.T. Vol. I, pamphlet 6, dealing in greater detail with this kind of training, has been issued to the Home Guard.

The training includes the following: (1) general principles and theory including warning, disposal of troops and formations for protection—non-movement, etc.,—maximum volume of controlled fire necessary, effective ranges, types of target—the direct attacker and the rover,—point of aim—the lead,—follow through or swing, use of tracer ammunition, recognition of aircraft, etc.; (2) exercises in fire discipline, aiming, recognition of aircraft, etc.; (3) actual practice firing with sub-caliber (22) on special targets; (4) demonstrations by planes detailed by R.A.F. for the purpose, etc.

For the exercises and actual firing certain accessories have been developed by the British: diagrams of enemy aircraft; diagrams of diving and climbing airplanes; model airplane with pole and stand fitted with moveable arm, rectangle and line-of-flight rod; spotlight projector (flashlight) apparatus with flex and transformer for fitting to rifle or light machine-gun; silhouette aircraft targets; moving target for use with the spotlight projector; special "lead" measurement markers and indicator on range or other suitable place; Model Dive Bomber Apparatus (developed at Osterly Park School and adopted by Home Guard). These will be described in detail in our Main Report.

Instruction No. 26 included directions which indicate some of the difficulties experienced by a country under service conditions; some British planes probably had been fired at by Home Guard who were too quick on the trigger:

"Opening fire on aircraft.

All Home Guards must be trained in anti-aircraft defense before being allowed to open fire on hostile aircraft, and this includes training in recognition of aircraft and behavior of aircraft.

Home Guard Training Instruction No. 17 gives clear information on this subject, and Home Guard commanders must ensure that all ranks are trained in A.A. defense and fully conversant with the details before they are allowed to open fire on hostile aircraft.

An aircraft will not be fired on unless:—
   i. it commits a hostile act
       or
   ii. it is definitely recognized as a hostile aircraft.

Fire will not be opened unless the target is within effective range of the weapons, and care should be taken to observe the second and subsequent waves of attacking aircraft to ensure that fire is not opened on our own fighters in pursuit of the enemy."

The Browning Automatic Rifle

The Browning Automatic Rifle: Home Guard Instruction No. 14 Appendix A sets out the standard for weapon training in the Browning Automatic Rifle. This arm is also mentioned in Instructions Nos. 18 and 26. For training purposes a War Office pamphlet "Instructional Notes On The .300-Inch Browning Automatic Rifle, 1940" has been issued to the Home Guard and pamphlets Nos. 1, 2 and 6 of the S.A.T. Vol. I series also deal with this arm as well as the rifle. The training follows that for the rifle except that such inherent subjects as "immediate action" are added and necessarily the firing courses on the range differ. These are covered in Instruction No. 14 Appendix A, which will be attached to our Main Report, together with the other official publications noted.

The Thompson Sub-Machine Gun

The Thompson Sub-Machine-Gun: The Home Guard were receiving their first sub-machine guns just when we were leaving England. To that date no actual training had taken place. There is a S.A.T. Vol. I pamphlet No. 21 on the Thompson Sub-Machine-Gun which we were told would be issued to the Home Guard as the basis for elementary training. It can be assumed that the training will in a general way follow that now used for the rifle and automatic rifle. The above pamphlet will be attached to our Main Report.

The Light Machine-Gun

The Light Machine-Gun: The arms of the Home Guard which fall properly within this classification are the Lewis, both air and water-cooled, and the Browning, air-cooled. The latter is our aircraft Browning, which is used by the Home Guard both for anti-aircraft work and as a ground light machine-gun. The Home Guard make the same anti-aircraft and ground use of the air-cooled aircraft Lewis.

In Home Guard Instruction No. 14, the directive for the 1940-41 Winter Training, the standards of training for the light machine-gun (Lewis) were set out and in Instruction No. 11 a firing course for light machine-guns is laid down. Care and cleaning were covered in Instruction No. 18. Pamphlets Nos. 1, 2, 3 and 6 of the S.A.T. Vol. I series deal in part with the use of and training with light machine-guns and pamphlet No. 20 of that series deals solely and specifically with the .303-inch Lewis Machine Gun. This same pamphlet was rewritten and issued later to cover small mechanical differences in the two arms as "Instructional Notes on the .300-Inch Lewis Machine Gun (Ground Action), 1940" and Instruction 20 states as to this pamphlet "This booklet applies to the Air Action .300-inch Lewis as well." All of these pamphlets have been issued to the Home Guard. They, together with the Home Guard Instructions mentioned, will be attached to our Main Report.

Again the training follows that for the rifle and automatic rifle with, of course, more emphasis on such matters as the mechanism, stoppages, immediate action, etc., because of the more complicated arm being dealt with. The training in tactical use naturally varies somewhat. The range firing course includes single rounds, normal rate and rapid fire up to 200 yards and on fixed and disappearing targets under the usual range control and discipline. Details will be given in our Main Report.

Machine Guns

Machine Guns (Water-cooled — tripod mounted): The first machine-guns issued to the Home Guard were the British Vickers .303-inch and they were not received until about the start of the 1940-41 winter training period. Home Guard Instruction No. 14, the directive for that period, is the first to deal with machine-gun training and is stated in terms of reference to Pamphlet No. 7 of the S.A.T. Vol. I series ".303-Inch Machine Gun." This pamphlet was issued to the regular forces in 1939 in three parts and a 1940 Supplement as follows: Part I—Mechanical Subjects; Part II—Training; Part III—Fire Control; Supplement—The Clinometer and Bar Foresight. Home Guard Instruction No. 14 does not refer to the Supplement, and states:

Instructions in this weapon will be given for direct firing only. Indirect fire and night firing will not be taught until proficiency is reached in direct fire and until the necessary instruments are available. Units armed with the M.G. should form M.G. sections."

The following covers in a general way the basic training given the Home Guard:

Mechanism—the gun and tripod;
General Maintenance—the gun and tripod;
Stripping;
Spare parts;
Stoppages and immediate action;
Repairs;
Instruments and aiming—tangent and fixed sights, elevation wheel, lamp aiming;
Elementary gun drill with certain standard tests;
Fire control (direct fire only) including general principles, fire orders, methods of fire, point targets, width targets, oblique targets, depth and area targets, moving targets;
Range practice up to 500 yards, fixed and traverse, single shot and bursts, on fixed patch targets, horizontal and oblique line targets and large convertible landscape targets.

Later Browning Machine-Guns were issued to the Home Guard. In this connection a War Office pamphlet "Instructional Notes on the .300-Inch Browning Machine Gun" was issued for training purposes. In Home Guard Instruction No. 26 certain minor amendments were made to the above pamphlet and there was added a description of the Model 1917 A.I. tripod. Except for the changes necessitated by the mechanical differences in the two guns and their tripods the training for the Browning is conducted on the same basis as that described above for the Vickers.

Pamphlets Nos. 1 and 2 of the S.A.T. Vol. I series also apply in part to machine-gun training. Several unofficial publications have been used by the Home Guard. A typical example is "The Browning Heavy Machine Gun" published by Gale and Polden. The above mentioned Instructions and pamphlets will be attached to our Main Report.

Grenades and Bombs

Grenades and Bombs: The analysis of the German tactics has shown that in addition to those factors mentioned above they have brought personal combat to close quarters. In implementing this they have emphasized the use of such short-range weapons as grenades, Tommy-guns and mortars, consequently in the British training to meet the German offensive tactics there is a like emphasis on such weapons which include grenades and bombs of various kinds. The grenade was early officially designated as an Home Guard weapon, Instruction No. 4. Its use against tanks was spoken of in Instruction No. 8. Instruction No. 9 dealt specifically and exclusively with grenades and laid down instructions for training, with particular emphasis on the No. 36, high explosive grenade, similar to our Mills. Instructions Nos. 11, 20 and 26 also touched on grenades. S.A.T. Vol. I Pamphlet No. 13 and Supplement No. 1, 1941, "Grenade," have been issued to the Home Guard and together with Instruction No. 9 are the basic instructions for training in grenades and bombs.

The Home Guard are issued and trained in the use of the following grenades and bombs:

No. 36 High Explosive (H.E.), similar to our Mills grenade, 1½ lbs., hand or rifle.

Smoke Grenade, 1¼ lbs., hand or rifle.

Day Signal Grenade, 1¼ lbs., hand or rifle.

Night Signal Grenade, 1¼ lbs., hand or rifle.

No. 69 Bakelite Grenade, light, not very destructive, for close up work, hand.

Anti-tank Petrol Bomb ("Molotov Cocktail"), incendiary, hand.

A.W. Grenade (Self-igniting, Phosphorus), incendiary, 1½ lbs., hand or Northover Projector.

S.T. Grenade ("Sticky"), high explosive, 2¼ lbs. (plus weight of cover, which is not thrown), hand, effective against armor up to 1 inch.

No. 68 Anti-tank Grenade, high-explosive, rifle.

No. 73 Hand Percussion Grenade (Anti-tank), high-explosive, about 4 lbs., hand.

No. 5 Smoke Bomb—3½ lbs., hand and mortar.

No. 15 Smoke Bomb—2¼ lbs., hand and mortar.

No. 10 Smoke Bomb—small, hand and mortar.

H.E. 2 inch Mortar Bomb, mortar.

Through necessity in the beginning many odd home-made grenades and bombs were made by or for the Home Guard. The later increased supply and issue of regulation grenades and bombs has made the use of such improvised weapons unnecessary and Instruction No. 26 provided:

"The grenades to be issued to the Home Guard will be restricted in due course to recognized Army types. Meanwhile the production of unauthorized home-made grenades must cease."

We do not understand that this prohibition extends to the "Molotov Cocktail," but recent evidence on improvements to German tanks has led the authorities to believe that its effectiveness has been greatly reduced.

The above list of grenades and bombs include some to be thrown by hand, some to be fired as rifle grenades, and some to be fired from projectors or mortars. The regular army rifle cup discharger is used, the issue 2 inch mortar and various types of home-made mortars, and a special projector, known as the Northover, for the A.W. grenade. The basic training includes the use of these projecting weapons as well as the different grenades and bombs. It, of course, includes a thorough course in the throwing of hand grenades. Training includes the following: safety precautions; stripping and assembling; mechanism; care and cleaning; aiming; throwing and firing, both dummy and live—sub and full charge-; tactical employment, including practice with smoke candles and grenades in working out effect of wind, the blinding of positions, etc.

The tactical use of grenades and bombs is covered in "Infantry Section Leading, 1938" and Military Training Pamphlet No. 42, "Tank Hunting and Destruction," both of which are issued to the Home Guard. Lectures on the subject and tactical exercises, using various types of dummy grenades (some containing chalk or flour so that a hit will be recorded), are included in the Home Guard training.

The above mentioned Instructions and Pamphlets with more detailed notes will be attached to and contained in our Main Report.

The Bayonet

The Bayonet: At first because of the lack of arms no question arose as to bayonet training for the Home Guard. The founders of the Osterly Park School and those who taught there took a very strong stand against bayonet training. Tom Wintringham, the founder of that school, said in August 1940, "The bayonet proved of little use in the American Civil War. It was ineffective in the Russo-Japanese War. It caused an infinitesimal number of the last war's casualties. Mechanization and automatic weapons leave it little scope. . . . The bayonet is a myth, a cult, a superstition that has no longer even a symbolic value. It may cheer the hearts of semi-decrepit politicians and even of much less decrepit generals to see the bayonets of the sentries in Whitehall. But to those of us who have had some fighting on a modern scale in recent years, the bayonet is a picturesque survival like the claymore or the battle-axe." This school of thought had a great deal of influence on the training of the individual Home Guard Units. On the other hand many former officers who are now commanders of Home Guard Units belong to the more conventional regular army school of thought and have given their units a certain amount of bayonet training. John Brophy, a widely read writer on Home Guard matters who has a regular column on Home Guard matters in the Sunday Graphic and News has taken an intermediate position. He states, "In this war the armies on both sides possess far more machine guns with a far higher fire power. And I suppose I need not tell anyone that it would be the most insane form of optimism to tackle a tank with a bayonet. All this seems to point unmistakably to the conclusion that the bayonet is obsolete. But the problem is not quite so simple as that. The Home Guard is not going to spend all its time charging at the enemy. It has to keep guard on thousands of posts throughout the country. It has to put out its sentries, especially by night. And there, I think, we can find a legitimate and important use for the bayonet. It is today first and foremost a sentry's weapon. On the one hand an enemy may creep up on the sentry in the darkness. . . . And that is where the bayonet on the muzzle of the rifle comes into its own. . . . But, used with proper skill, it will enable him to make sure no enemy knifes him or strangles him—and the quiet dispatch of a sentry before he can raise an alarm is always a big advantage to an approaching enemy. That, as I see it, is the chief justification for the retention of the bayonet as a weapon of modern warfare."

In the Home Guard Instruction No. 14 there was set out a "SEQUENCE OF BAYONET TRAINING INSTRUCTION," which included three lessons, following the usual type of bayonet training common to all armies and necessitating the use of dummies and the Training Stick. There has also been issued to the Home Guard S.A.T. Vol. I Pamphlet No. 12 which is the regular army manual on the bayonet.

The Pistol and Revolver

The Pistol and Revolver: When we asked an Home Guard Instructor what he thought was the proper range for training the Home Guard in the use of the pistol and revolver, he answered, "As far as they can reach and if the enemy is further than that I advise them to throw the weapon at the enemy." This is perhaps extreme, but it is indicative. Some officers and non-commissioned officers of the Home Guard are armed with this weapon. There is no mention of the weapon in the Home Guard Instructions, except that in Instruction No. 20 it is provided that at the discretion of Area or Battalion Commanders one copy of S.A.T. Vol. I Pamphlet 11 "Pistol (.38-inch)" may be issued to each company of the Home Guard. From our observations there has certainly been very little training in the use of this arm.

Use of Flame

Use of Flame: The use of flame from a mixture of burning gasoline and oil against an enemy is planned and practiced by the Home Guard. In most cases it is planned as an anti-tank or anti-armored vehicle measure.

In the simplest form gasoline and oil is spread on a road and ignited. In suitable conditions the intense heat and flame will result in the destruction or immobilization of enemy vehicles. This use is restricted to defiles which the enemy are likely to use. Both gravity or pump from a reservoir hidden and protected at a distance but from within view of the defile are used to place the inflammable mixture on the road. The tank of mixture may either be static or mobile. This method is covered in Military Training Pamphlet No. 42 which is issued to the Home Guard. This pamphlet will be attached to our Main Report.

A second method is known as the "Fougasse." This method can be used in a defile or where there is at least one high bank at the side of the road. Barrels of the inflammable mixture are buried in the bank with charges directly behind them. When the enemy vehicles are in a proper position the charges are ignited by electricity and the barrels are blown out of the bank onto the road dousing the vehicles with the inflammable mixture which is set off by the explosion of the charge.

Another method is really an adaptation of the Fougasse. It is known as the "Hedge-Hopper." In this case the barrels are placed behind a hedge or wall which lines the road at a proper angle and with explosive charges under them. Again when the enemy vehicles are in the proper place on the road the charges are set off and the barrels of inflammable mixture hurtle over the hedge or wall landing on the road and vehicles as a mass of flaming liquid.

Another method of using flame is with flame-throwers. There are two different types issued to the Home Guard, one known as the "Harvey" and the other as the "Home Guard." In the case of the "Harvey" the liquid is expelled from a cylinder through a hose and nozzle by pressure furnished from a nitrogen flask attached to the cylinder. In the case of the "Home Guard" flame-thrower the pressure is furnished by a hand pump. These flame-throwers are designed mainly as defensive equipment for fixed road blocks and are sited on the flank on the enemy side of the road block. The "Harvey" is described in Military Training Pamphlet No. 42 and the "Home Guard" in a pamphlet issued by the Petroleum Department (which we were never able to obtain). The tactical use of flame-throwers is covered in M.T.P. 42. Both are issued to the Home Guard.

Land Mines and Tank Traps

Land Mines and Tank Traps: A few members of the Home Guard Units are trained in the use of land mines and tank traps based on such mines. These men are trained in the mechanism, the laying, etc., of the mines. The British Army have training mines which when "exploded" emit a cloud of smoke-like vapor. These are used in exercises. More will be said of this subject in connection with Tank Hunting and Destruction. Military Training Pamphlet No. 40 "Anti-Tank Mines" and Military Training Pamphlet No. 42 dealing with their tactical use have been issued to the Home Guard.

Booby Traps

Booby Traps: Booby traps is the name given to small improvised contact mines and charges placed in buildings, pill boxes, trenches, dead ground, etc., to render their occupation dangerous. The Home Guard are generally trained in their use. More will be said of them in connection with Guerrilla Warfare. Field Engineering Pamphlet No. 9, 1941

"Booby Traps and Tank Traps" has been issued to the Home Guard, and will be attached to our Main Report.

NOTE: From our conversation and investigations it seemed apparent to us that the British will furnish the Home Guard with both the Anti-Tank Rifle, Calibre .55-Inch (see S.A.T. Vol. I Pamphlet No. 5 which will be attached to our Main Report) and the Anti-Tank Gun, a 2 pounder when they are available.

First Aid

First Aid: The Home Guard is given training in elementary first aid. This subject is mentioned in the official Instructions and Pamphlets only in Home Guard Instruction No. 14 where it is laid down as one of the subjects to be studied during the 1940-41 Winter Training Period.

Gas

Gas: In Home Guard Instruction No. 5 Anti-Gas Training is included as one of the necessary elements of training for the Home Guard and in Instruction No. 14, the training directive for the 1940-41 Winter Training Period, it is stated as one of the subjects to be studied and in Appendix A a standard for training is set out. Instruction No. 24 deals specifically and exclusively with protection against gas. It sets out a comprehensive plan for anti-gas training, including general description of the characteristics of the gasses, of protective measures and of anti-gas equipment. It sets up a series of gas alarms and signals. It describes the care and cleaning of gas masks, provides for the inspection of masks and their fitting. It includes a gas mask drill and finally sets up a test for elementary training. Anti-gas measures are also touched upon in a general way in the following official publications issued to the Home Guard: Military Training Pamphlet No. 23 Part IV Protection, 1939 and Infantry Section Leading, 1938. Field Service Pocketbook Pamphlet No. 8 also issued to the Home Guard deals specifically and exclusively with protection against gas. This goes further than Instruction No. 24 in that it provides for the protection of houses, posts, dug-outs, pill boxes, etc. in addition to personnel protection.

Military Training Pamphlet No. 23 Part V "The Use of Gas in the Field" and Military Training Pamphlet No. 32 Part VI "Bombs, Ground, 6-lb." both deal with the affirmative use of gas and are issued to the Home Guard. Both have the following introduction: "The British Government has no intention of initiating the use of gas. The British Army must, however, be prepared to protect itself against the use of gas by an enemy. A study of the methods by which gas might be employed in the field is therefore necessary, but such methods would only be adopted by the British Army if it were decided that retaliatory measures were required."

All of the members of the Home Guard are equipped with gas masks and are trained along the lines set out in Instruction No. 24 with lectures, demonstrations, drill and tests. They are also practiced in the protection of their posts, pill boxes, etc. against gas. We know of no training of the Home Guard in the affirmative use of gas.

The above mentioned Instructions and Pamphlets will be attached to our Main Report.

Fieldcraft

Fieldcraft: (The terms Fieldcraft and Scouting are to some degree used synonymously in the instruction of the Home Guard.)

It is obvious that to send troops, armed only as the Home Guard necessarily must be, against German tanks, dive-bombers and motorized infantry, supported by mobile field and medium artillery, would be murder except for the fact that the Home Guard is operating in its own back yard, which it knows better than anyone else including the enemy, and which it can prepare in advance so as to furnish it the greatest possible protection.

This leads us to two training subjects which are basic to the Home Guard—Fieldcraft and Field Fortification. Both of these subjects involve the knowledge and the practical application of Concealment and Camouflage.

In Military Training Pamphlet No. 33—1940 "Training in Fieldcraft and Elementary Tactics", issued to the Home Guard, appears the following definition—

"Fieldcraft is the use of natural cover and conditions in conjunction with movement and the employment of weapons. It is the art of the hunter and includes concealment, silent movement, knowledge of his prey and skill with his weapons."

This is the basic, training publication on the subject.

"Infantry Section Leading, 1938", a pamphlet which is also issued to the Home Guard, has a section on Fieldcraft. The first paragraph gives this definition—

"The term fieldcraft includes initiative, cunning and intelligence in the use of ground so that a soldier may arrive on his objective alive and fit to fight."

Fieldcraft deals then, amongst other things, with cover from view and fire; types of cover; how to use cover; camouflage; keeping direction; and moving by night, in mist, or in smoke.

NOTE: Paragraphs on Concealment and Camouflage follow below.

As the functions of the Home Guard developed to meet the ever extending role required of the Force (to warn, to delay, to harrass), the subject of Fieldcraft became a necessary part of the Home Guard training. Instructions Nos. 4 and 8 called for Training in Fieldcraft. Instruction No. 14 "Winter Training" directed that lecture courses, etc. be given on this subject. Home Guard Instruction No. 22 "Guides" is a related Instruction.

Night Training is given an important place in Home Guard instruction. Instruction No. 4, 1940 has as its opening paragraph under "Night" the following—"Man is a day animal. War requires that he should become a night fighter." Home Guard Instruction No. 10 gives a special section under "Night Operations." Home Guard Instruction No. 23 is devoted entirely to Night Training:

"The object of night training is to develop a night sense in the individual so as to give him confidence and increase his efficiency in observation and movement ... Training to achieve this object must be carefully graded and progressive. The first essential is to bring to their most acute sensitiveness the senses of sight, hearing and touch ... When the keenness of the three senses by night has been stimulated and the efficiency of the man in observation increased by (certain designated) exercises, training in movement by night should be given."

There are issued as well by the War Office pamphlets dealing directly or indirectly on this subject which are used in Home Guard Training, such as:

Military Training Pamphlet No. 37, 1940 "The Training of an Infantry Batallion";

Pamphlet, "Training and War, Infantry Training, 1937";

Pamphlet "Infantry Training 1937, Supplement, Tactical Notes for Platoon Commanders", 1941;

Notes on May Reading 1929 (Reprint with amendments (Nos. 1-4) 1939). This includes detailed data on the use of the Compass.

Field Service Pocketbook, Pamphlet No. 3, 1939, "Intelligence Information and Security";

Official Pamphlet, "The Home Guard Can Fight" by Wintringham;

Military Training Pamphlet No. 42, 1940 "Tank Hunting and Destruction."

Other semi-official pamphlets dealing with these subjects, such as, "The Home Guard Training Manual" by Langdon-Davies, "Home Guard for Victory" by Hugh Slater, "New Ways of War by Wintringham, are recommended by the War Office in Home Guard Instruction No. 26.

NOTE: The above pamphlets will be available as exhibits in our Main Report.

The Training in Fieldcraft is given an important place in the training at the War Office Schools for Home Guard Instructors, as well as among the Home Guard Units themselves.

Training by Lectures, Pamphlets, etc.

Training: (a) By lectures, pamphlets, etc.:
1. Emphasis on knowledge of locality and local population.
2. Knowledge of camouflage of clothing, observation points, hiding places, etc.
3. What nature has to offer in concealment (view and fire cover), and warnings—pro and con.
4. Knowledge of proper movement—how, where and when to move.
5. Development of hearing—with proper interpretation of sound—by day and by night.
6. Development of sight with proper interpretation of what is seen by day and by night.
7. Development of sense of smell—with proper interpretation.
8. Knowledge of scouting corelated with knowledge of guiding.
9. Appreciation of accuracy of understanding and repetition of "Verbal Orders." "A verbal order must be short and clear ... should be spoken clearly, slowly and without hesitation."

10. Practical weapons to carry and how to use them.
11. Knowledge of buildings and how, when and where to move—over, around or through them.
12. What to expect and guard against.

Note: Covered in detail in our Main Report with instruction pamphlets, etc., as Exhibits.

Training by Exercises

Training: (b) by Exercises:
1. Game of observation where a selected group take up their positions in full sight with a background of natural cover. "Fading into the landscape."
2. How to walk.
3. How to crawl (with or without weapons).
4. "Grandmother's Footsteps." Game of moving when "Grandmother's" head is turned. Home Guard must not be detected in movement.
5. German Sentry—(blindfolded to represent night.) Home Guard approach without being detected. When detected Home Guard is "killed" and out of game.
6. Night exercises testing sense of sight—hearing—sound—touch.
7. Games that test accuracy of delivering "verbal messages."

Concealment and Camouflage

Concealment and Camouflage:

"It should not be assumed that concealment and camouflage are applicable only to field engineering. They are equally important in every form of military activity in the field."

The above is the introductory note in Military Training Pamphlet No. 26, 1939 on Concealment and Camouflage, which pamphlet is issued to Home Guard Commanders and Instructors. The pamphlet further states,—

"Concealment is a matter of common sense and of good discipline."

"All ranks ... must be made to realize the importance of avoiding recognition, not only by enemy ground and air observers, but also by detection in enemy air photographs."

"Concealment does not end with the individual; it is equally important to conceal bodies of troops, weapons, vehicles, works of defence, etc."

From the training point of view concealment is divided into:
(1) Individual concealment of fieldcraft and scoutcraft;
(2) Collective concealment, i.e. the concealment of bodies of troop units and formations;
(3) Concealment of field works, weapons and vehicles;
(4) Concealment from the air, particularly against the camera.

No. 4 applies equally to the first three, and is of tremendous importance today. Tanks, infantry and all arms have their accompanying air-craft which attempt to clear the way for them.

Military Training Pamphlet No. 30, 1940 "Field Engineering (All Arms) Part II, Notes on Screens," covers the following general subjects: Employment of Screens; Conditions of effectiveness; Materials and types of Screens; Opacity; Visibility; Siting of Road Screens; Flash Screens and Manufacture—Direction and Maintenance. (This pamphlet includes designs and illustrations.)

While the "Home Guard Instructions" have dealt with these subjects only indirectly, other printed pamphlets or booklets (such as the "Home Guard Training Manual" by Langdon-Davies), the War Office Schools, and Home Guard Instructors have treated Concealment and Camouflage as important.

Training in Concealment and Camouflage through Lectures and Pamphlets

Training in Concealment and Camouflage through
(a) Lectures and Pamphlets:
   (1) "The Airplane is the eye of the modern army"—therefore great need and importance of Concealment and Camouflage.
   (2) Concealment and camouflage of weapons, action stations, headquarters, cars, trucks, etc., within and without a village.
   (3) Knowledge of color—tone—texture—shadow—materials—clothing—nets, etc., as applied to camouflage.
   (4) Concealment and camouflage in nature, and what can be learned from animal and still life.
   (5) Good and poor camouflage.
   (6) What is obvious from the air and from the ground—telltale tracks, etc.
   (7) Concealment and camouflage of movements; individual, in units, afoot and in vehicles.
   (8) Special application to observers—scouts—guerilla warfare.
   (9) Discipline.
   (10) Maintenance.

Training in Concealment and Camouflage through Exercises

Training in Concealment and Camouflage through
(b) Exercises.

These exercises are practiced in the major part in connection with training in Fieldcraft, Patrols, Scouting and Guerrilla Warfare. Also practice on concealment and camouflage is constantly given to the Home Guard in its current work of siting and preparing its field fortifications.

Actual tests and demonstrations in:
   (1) Camouflaged clothing and weapons applied to troops.
   (2) Special nets as camouflage for parked cars (this will be enlarged upon in our Main Report), observation posts, etc.
   (3) Application of color and special materials.
   (4) Effect of tones, shadows, etc.
   (5) Tests in cooperating with nature.

Field Fortification

Field Fortification: The object of Field Fortification should be the development by artificial means of natural "cover from view" and natural "cover from fire."

While it is primarily the duty of the "regular" military forces to plan and site the field fortifications to be manned by the Home Guard, many times as a practical matter the question of time and availability automatically placed this responsibility on the Home Guard.

At first, owing to the emergency of the situation and the scarcity of time and because the subject of concealment and camouflage were ignored or not understood, many errors were made by the Home Guard in designing and siting of field fortifications. Thus the importance of a knowledge and the application of concealment and camouflage became apparent. Today, however, these errors are fast being corrected and turned to advantage by using ill-sited positions and field works as dummy or decoy targets.

The duties assigned to the Home Guard by Instructions Nos. 1, 2 and 4, indicated that knowledge of the elements of field fortification was required of that Force. Instruction No. 7, "Notes on Field Defences," dealt specifically and exclusively with this subject. It covered such subjects as sand-bagging; protection against small arms fire, thickness of various materials required; weapon pits; breast works; slit trenches; concealment; defenses of a village. No. 12 applied No. 7 to factory defense. No. 14, the Directive for the 1940-41 Winter Training Period, enumerated "Elementary Field Fortification" as one of the subjects to be studied and in Appendix A fixed a standard of training.

Infantry Training, 1937 (Sect. 74, 8 and Appendix IV) has many good hints on Field Fortification, though the organization of positions is too linear and not sufficient weight is given to cover from the air. The 1941 Supplement to this pamphlet, "Tactical Notes for Platoon Commanders" Part II, goes a long way in correcting these faults and gives many good hints on the siting, organizing and fortifying of defense positions. Field Service Pocketbook, Pamphlet No. 4, as Amended, 1940, "Field Engineering," covers in greater detail than Instruction No. 7 the construction of Field Fortifications. It covers generally the following: simple field geometry; tools; materials; factors governing the design of protective works; field defense works; preparation of buildings, walls, hedges, etc. for defence; obstacles; concealment and camouflage. Military Training Pamphlet No. 30 Part III, "Obstacles," deals with the construction of all kinds of obstacles, including amongst others the following: low wire entanglement; cattle fence; triple concertina fence; double apron fence; portable knife rest; concertina road block; movable lorry block; felled trees; concrete cylinders; buoys (called "dollies" by the Home Guard); pimples (called "dragon's teeth" by the Home Guard); rail barrier; use of bullheaded 90-lb. rails; use of flat-bottom, 90-lb. rails; protection of rail barrier by sandbags; bent rails (called "hair pins" by the Home Guard); cable tank block; anti-tank ditch; scarped slope; scarped slope and logs; natural steep slope and logs; bank and log; barricade timber walls; anti-tank ditch revetment; ditch in soft ground; ditch in wet ground and ditch in hard ground. One of the materials used in Field Fortification is the Dannert Concertina of wire. A "Concertina" is a coil of barbed wire which, when pulled out like the musical instrument from which it takes its name, retains its round coiled shape. There are three pamphlets on the use of this form of wire as an obstacle, Military Training Pamphlets No. 21, 21 A, and 21 B. All of the above Instructions and Pamphlets are issued to the Home Guard and will be included as exhibits in our Main Report.

The training of the Home Guard in Field Fortification is implemented by lectures, assigned reading in the above pamphlets, demonstrations and they have continuous practice in the preparation and organization of their own defensive positions which includes the use of weapon pits, crawl trenches, slit trenches, pill boxes, road blocks, the fortifying of buildings, loop-holing, wiring, etc.

The use of camouflage in connection with the training and practice of the Home Guard in Field Fortification is greatly emphasized, for further details see above.

Tactical Training

Tactical Training: We now come to the training of the Home Guard in the tactical application of those basic subjects the training in which we have reviewed above.

Minor Tactics

Minor Tactics: Though the Home Guard from a strategical point of view is static, in its own area of operations it is locally very mobile. This area for any unit is necessarily restricted to short distances from the homes or working places of the Unit's members. But its peculiar local knowledge of the area and its consequent high mobility in the area are two of the factors that render it an effective force. Before taking up those special duties, such as the pinning down of parachute troops, the manning of road-blocks, etc., which fall peculiarly within the mission of the Home Guard, it should be noted that that force is trained in the usual minor tactics for small units, offensive, defensive, security, etc. In fact great emphasis in the training of the Home Guard is placed on the development of the initiative and independence of action of individuals and small units.

This subject is covered in the Home Guard training by lectures and both outdoor and indoor exercises. "Infantry Section Leading, 1938," which outlines some of the principles of minor tactics for small units, is referred to in Instructions Nos. 20 and 23. The following pamphlets which also touch on minor tactics are issued to the Home Guard: "Infantry Training—Training and War, 1937" and its 1941 supplement, "Tactical Notes for Platoon Commanders"; Military Training Pamphlet No. 37, 1940, "The Training of an Infantry Battalion". Instruction No. 21 deals specifically and exclusively with "Indoor Tactical Training" with the use of sand and cloth models. The Home Guard did a lot of this kind of work with models and the magnetic blackboard, including command exercises, known in England as T.W.E.Ts, particularly during the 1940-41 Winter Training Period.

Special Tactical Roles

Special Tactical Roles: As stated above in Section D on Tactics (p. 18) the original conception of the Home Guard was of a force to confine the operations of German parachutists, other air-borne troops, and then any tanks or other armored vehicles which the Germans might be able to land. The opening sentence of Instruction No. 1 is "Enemy parachutists or air-borne troops may commandeer vehicles and then try to seize important localities with speed." The first three instructions were really operational directives, No. 4 being the first to deal with training, and they really dealt with the tactics to be employed to accomplish this "confining" job of the Home Guard. Anti-parachute (including other air-landed troops) and anti-tank (including other armored vehicles) operations are still two of the important jobs of the Home Guard.

Anti-Air Troops

Anti-Air Troops (Including Parachutists and Other Air-Landed Troops): Instruction No. 2 provided for watchers for parachute landings, stating:

"Any such watch himself seeing the descent of enemy parachutists in his neighborhood will broadcast the alarm by ringing church bells. The bells will not be rung for any other purpose. He will NOT repeat the alarm given from a neighboring church, since this will only confuse the issue as to where the parachutists have landed. Besides broadcasting the alarm, watchers will at once report what they have seen as in the case of active defense detachments. It is only by ensuring that all probable areas of attack are under constant observation that early news of enemy landings can be guaranteed."

NOTE: Though Instruction No. 2 has been replaced by No. 10, the ringing of church bells is still the designated signal for landing of enemy air-borne troops.

Instruction No. 2 also provided for "active defence (counter parachute) detachments" who were to "engage and report enemy parachutists." As Appendix B, it had "Notes On German Parachutists." These "Notes" describe the German Parachutists, their equipment and arms, their mission and tactics, including the jump. It gives instructions for counter-measures. It states:

"Germans, who have made a study of the subject, say that the only defence against parachutists is the active and collective co-operation of the population, who need systematic and intelligent instruction. In the Local Defence Volunteer Force this need has been met."

NOTE: It is difficult to see how "the active and collective cooperation of the population" against parachutists can be obtained without the formation of some such force as the Home Guard, because any one attacking parachutists would be breaking the laws of war and would be franctireurs, if captured, unless they were properly enrolled in some such military force.

These "Notes" of Instruction No. 2 were amplified and rewritten, with five sections, as Instruction No. 3. There were attached 4 plates

41

illlustrating the parachute troops and some of their equipment and arms. This Instruction, together with a reprint of one of the Osterly Park lectures contained in a pamphlet, "The Home Guard Can Fight," officially published and distributed to the Home Guard, still are the basis for the instruction of units of that force in the tactics to be used against parachutists and air-landed troops. Instructions No. 5 and 7 and the official pamphlet "Tactical Notes for Platoon Commanders," 1941 added a couple of minor details. To summarize:

During the jump the parachutist carries a few weapons—a revolver, one in five a machine pistol, a few grenades and a spring-knife. Other weapons are dropped separately in containers, including rifles, sub-machine guns, machine guns, ammunition, etc. The jump is from about 300 feet. The men are about five seconds in the air (7 seconds according to certain information from Crete). The descent is rapid and at irregular speeds, the latter due to the different degrees of openness of the parachute. Consequently the men are bad targets in the air. The parachute itself is not injured by bullet holes. Instruction No. 5 pointed out that the parachute should not be fired at. Twelve men or cases can leave the plane in ten seconds. They should fall in a minimum area of 400 square yards. For action they must therefore assemble. It takes thirty seconds for the men to get out of their parachute harness. It has been reported that it takes from eight to twelve minutes for the men to recover from the shock of landing, get their arms from the containers, and assemble as organized fighting units. The attack, if advisable, is best made on the parachutists in that eight to twelve minutes. The very best is, of course, the first thirty seconds. The next best before the men get to the containers. Fire may be directed at either men or containers which are packed with arms and explosives and are vulnerable to small arms fire, grenades, etc.

The first duty of the Home Guard is to warn of the landing. If there are sufficient members present this need not occupy all of the unit. The Home Guard should not attack, unless, under all the circumstances, it has an even chance of wiping out the parachutists. If a quick summing up of the situation seems to indicate such a chance, action must be immediate and should be concurrent with the sending off of a warning. If no attack should be made the duty of the Home Guard is to shadow the parachutists and snipe at them, sending information back occasionally so as to permit the regular military authorities to know currently where the enemy is.

The Home Guard handles other air-landed troops in a similar way to parachutists, but it also has the passive duty of erecting obstructions on likely landing places. Originally many of these obstructions were planned and erected in the form of ditches, holes, piles of earth, banks, etc. Latterly it was recognized that though such obstructions would be effective against fighters and light bombers, they would do little damage to large, heavy transports, such as are usually used for crash landings, and the subsequent normal landings of air-borne troops. Consequently strong wires stretched at appropriate heights, heavy posts or concrete blocks placed at appropriate intervals, etc., have been used in obstructing possible landing places. Such landing places include open fields, golf links, broad highways, etc., as well as prepared landing fields.

The tactical training of the Home Guard in its duties against air-landed troops is taught by lectures, field exercises, etc.

Many of the unofficial manuals, etc. deal with parachute and air-landed troops. The following are some of them:

The Home Guard Training Manual—Langdon-Davis—p. 137.
Home Guard—A Handbook—Brophy—pp. 21, 30, and 42.
Hints for the Home Guard—Fitzwilliams—p. 40.
Home Guard Pocket Book—Green—p. 71.

All of the above Instructions, Pamphlets, Manuals, etc., will be available as exhibits with our main report.

Tank Destruction

Tank Destruction (Including other armored vehicles): In Military Training Pamphlet No. 42, 1940, "Tank Hunting And Destruction" (issued to the Home Guard) appears the following:

"Every soldier and every member of the Home Guard should be trained in the methods of tank hunting and in the use of special anti-tank weapons. The lessons of Spain and Finland confirm that tanks can be destroyed by men who have the bravery, resource and determination to do so."

Tank Destruction tactically falls into two main phases, active and passive. The British speak of the active phase as "Tank Hunting." The passive phase includes the use of Road Blocks, tank obstacles, minefields, ambushes, and is one of the elements of Village Defense, etc. Certain training is common to both phases. First, the study of German tanks and other armored vehicles so that they may be recognized and so that their weaknesses and vulnerability may be understood. Also the study of anti-tank weapons and training in their use (this has been covered above in the paragraphs on weapon training).

Instruction No. 8 "Tanks and Tank Destruction" and Military Training Pamphlet No. 42, spoken of above, which together are the basic directives for the Home Guards' operations and training in anti-tank work, both describe German tanks, their weaknesses and vulnerable points. The weaknesses include: blindness; limited field of fire; vulnerability of tracks; hardship on crews and consequent necessity of rest; limited gasoline supply; immobility in dark. The vulnerable points include: driver's, gunner's and commander's slits (to small arms fire, grenades, use of flame); belly and top of tank (to anti-tank rifle, special high-explosive anti-tank bombs, mines); tracks (to anti-tank rifle, special high-explosive anti-tank grenades, mines and the bogies possibly to flame); louvres or air vents (to incendiary grenades and bombs); turret when open, which will be as much as tank crew dare (to small arms fire, grenades and bombs—both high-explosive and incendiary—all by surprise). The use of both high-explosive and incendiary grenades and bombs against tanks in either phase must be from very close quarters, though the distance is extended by the use of the rifle-cup discharger, mortars and Northover projector.

Tank Hunting

Tank Hunting: Instruction No. 8, "Tanks and Tank Destruction" starts with paragraph 1. "The Task. From the moment that enemy tanks are located they must be harried, hunted, sniped, and ambushed without respite until they are destroyed. Goliath was slain by David's sling, and the lessons of Spain and Finland confirm that tanks can be destroyed by men who have the bravery, resource, and determination to do so."

Military Training Pamphlet No. 42, 1940, "Tank Hunting and Destruction," says: "Tank hunting must be regarded as a sport—big game hunting at its best. A thrilling, albeit a dangerous sport, which if skillfully played is about as hazardous as shooting tiger on foot, and in which the same principles of stalk and ambush are followed."

The training of the Home Guard in "Tank Hunting" is carried out by assigned reading in the above pamphlet, by lectures which point out, amongst other things: the vulnerability of tanks; the necessity of temporarily stopping their movement; the necessity of getting to close quarters to destroy or immobilize them; the blindness and limited field of fire of tanks which make close up safer than distance; use of smoke and incendiary grenades as cover and to blind tanks for close approach; convergence from different angles while watching tank's guns and using cover; attacks on tanks when crews are resting, particularly when "harboring" at night; methods of demobilizing and rendering unserviceable captured tanks, etc. Most of the training is included in that on the basic subjects of fieldcraft, scouting, use of weapons, etc., but special exercises in stalking and getting to close quarters with tanks are carried on.

Tank Destruction— Passive Phase

Tank Destruction—Passive Phase: One operation of the Home Guard is on the borderline between the active and passive phases of tank or armored vehicle destruction, namely, ambushing. In view of the fact that to ambush successfully armored vehicles it is necessary that the ambushes be reconnoitered and planned in advance and that it is often desirable that the necessary material be placed ready nearby, such operations partake of the characteristics of the passive phase. On the other hand fixed positions, such as are involved in road blocks, are not prepared. The variations of an ambush are almost unlimited. The essence of a good ambush is surprise; it cannot therefore be made a subject for rules. They must therefore be devised and planned through the ingenuity of the individual leaders who must pit their wits against those of the enemy in making such plans. The object must always be to mystify and mislead. Obvious places should not be chosen. Suitable places will, however, generally be found in defiles, such as cuttings between banks, woods, and even villages and towns. The following are some of the points to be considered in making plans:

(a) That tanks are often preceded by a fringe of motor-cyclists and light armored vehicles;

(b) To surprise and overcome the reconnoitering motor-cyclists before they are able to warn the leading tank. A wire stretched taut across the road 3 feet from the ground will often be sufficient. If possible, these motor-cyclists should be disposed of silently, and devices for puncturing their tires will sometimes be useful (e.g., boards with upturned nails, broken glass, etc.);

(c) To attack tanks individually and to prevent them supporting each other. Bends in the roads may make this possible; if not, one alternative is to make use of smoke bombs to isolate individual tanks. Having isolated a tank it may be attacked with incendiary bombs and high explosive grenades until it is destroyed. In village streets, woods and other narrow defiles speed of action, surprise and a simultaneous attack on supporting tanks may render the isolation of individual tanks unnecessary;

(d) The provision of "look-outs" to protect the ambushing detachments from motorized infantry following the tanks. The action of the enemy infantry when the leading tanks have met an ambush is likely to be to deploy with the intention of taking the ambushers in flank or rear.

(e) Arrangements for the withdrawal of the party and getting them once more under control so that they may prepare fresh ambushes and continue the fight. These arrangements include the selection of a rendezvous (which should be known to every man), the parking of vehicles, bicycles, etc., with a view to the "get-away" and signals for withdrawal.

Road Blocks

Road Blocks: As stated above tanks are generally preceded by a fringe of motor-cycle scouts and accompanied by lightly armored vehicles. The passive phase of the destruction of these armored vehicles involves the manning of various kinds of prepared positions and the destruction of the vehicles by the proper use of various arms from those positions. The commonest form of this kind of position is the Road Block. Any position designed to stop tanks must be very strongly constructed because tanks are so powerful that they can break through anything but the strongest obstructions. We will have more to say of this later. On the other hand much lighter obstructions will serve to stop the motor-cycles and light armored cars. Every possible device should be used to slow up the movement of enemy mobile columns. Motor cyclists, though often a difficult target when on the move, are very vulnerable when halted. The defence has achieved much if it can make the task of the reconnoitering motor cyclists so dangerous that the tanks themselves must lead the column. The purpose is to instil into the enemy such a fear of ambushes that he will approach every defile and bend in the road with caution. A great advantage will have been obtained if the enemy has been forced to make a reconnaissance before attempting to pass such points. The following have been found to be effective to stop motor-cycles and light armored vehicles: cratering of road with explosives; ditching or trenching across road; barricading with local materials such as loaded farm carts, old automobiles, debris, etc.; felled trees; light "knife rests" (wooden frames covered with barbed wire); concertinas; for motor-cycles only, as mentioned above, a single wire stretched across a road three feet from the ground; fakes—the surface of the road broken up as though the road had been mined or even a row of upturned soup plates, a number of blankets slung across a village street, strips of canvas laid across a road as if to conceal a trench or booby trap, hay or straw spread over a stretch of road—; broken glass; booby traps of different kinds, such as small road mines, charges for felling trees, bombs designed to burst in the foliage of trees above tanks and set off by a trip wire across the road, bombs designed to fall on vehicles which set them off by a trip wire, etc.

As stated above, to be effective against tanks, road blocks must be very strongly constructed and of a permanent nature, consequently, the siting of such road blocks is a matter for the regular army commander of the disrict in which they are to be built, otherwise, such permanent road blocks might interfere with the movement of the regular field forces. (See Instructions Nos. 2 and 10).

Home Guard Instruction No. 1 stated that "Road blocks should be built at points where it is difficult for drivers of approaching vehicles:
   i. To see the obstacle until they are close to it.
   ii. To turn the vehicle around.
   iii. To drive off the road and move across country.

Hence defiles where the road passes between woods, deep ditches, thick hedges or buildings are suitable. Surprise should be obtained by choosing a site round a corner, where the block will be invisible until the hostile vehicles are almost on top of it." Instructions No. 4 and 10 point out that the enemy will attempt to outflank a road block and that the Home Guard should plan to prevent it. Consequently the ability to organize a road block for all around defence must be considered in siting it. Instruction No. 8 and Military Training Pamphlet No. 42, "Tank Hunting and Destruction" and Military Training Pamphlet No. 30, "Obstacles" also bear on this question of siting. In addition to the above the following are some of the factors affecting the siting of road blocks:

   Closed down, a tank is blind immediately overhead and on the ground within 15 feet. It is an advantage therefore if the points at which the tanks are stopped are overlooked at close range by banks or second floor windows, roofs, etc. so that the tanks can be bombed from above, or by roadside cover such as ditches, buildings, etc. so that bombs can be thrown at or rails pushed into the tracks from positions close to tanks at ground level.

Fire from a tank is impossible on the ground within about 20 feet or at an elevation above a tank greater than 25 degrees. The restricted field of fire of tanks has the same influence on the siting of road blocks as their blindness.

Danger of blind spots and dead angles from fire being covered by view or fire of other tanks, therefore, obstruction should be sited just around a bend.

Because of the fixed fire from the tank's arms various positions at various angles for simultaneous attack should be provided.

Tank cannot fire into slit trenches (deep and narrow) at any range except in enfilade, consequently such trenches advisable in organizing the attacking points and the defensive system of a road block. To meet the possibility of enfilade fire the "cross trench" or bays in straight trenches should be provided.

It is impossible to tell from which side of the road block the enemy may approach, consequently it must be organized for all around defence. The possibility of all around defence should be considered in siting the road block.

The possibility of closing the side of the block with natural obstacles or barbed wire to keep the enemy dismounted personnel in view and range of the defenders should be considered in siting the road block.

Occasionally, if the road passes through long defiles, it may be possible to provide for the dropping of an obstacle behind the enemy in the defile.

One of the most important elements in determining the siting of road blocks is the possibility of camouflaging or obtaining cover from the air.

Obstacles to stop tanks are very difficult to design. Tanks have great power of overcoming obstacles by their momentum, particularly if they can charge at speed. For instance, a 25 ton tank travelling at 13 to 14 miles per hour can pass almost unchecked through three rows of 70-lb. rails which project vertically above the road surface at 5 feet spacing. Obstacles should be designed to absorb the momentum of the tank by lifting it up rather than by bringing it to a dead stop. It must also be remembered that tanks destroy obstacles by fire from their own armament. The penetration into good concrete of a single shot from a 2 pounder from a range of about 80 yards may be as much as 30 inches. Small concrete blocks are disintegrated by a single shot and 4 foot reinforced concrete cubes can be destroyed by a dozen shots. The obstruction in the road block should be planned to include devices for slowing the tank's rate of advance before it reaches the main obstacle. The series of obstacles should be concealed by some sort of camouflage such as canvas screens, garnished netting, brush wood, old vehicles used as decoys, etc. so that the true nature of the series of obstacles as a whole may be hidden and so that the most vulnerable parts will not be obvious to the enemy and consequently subject to accurate fire.

If the tank can be forced to stop to investigate, the defence must at once sieze the opportunity of taking offensive action to destroy it. Anti-tank mines can be combined to great advantage with the elements of the obstruction. The following are some of the elements that may be combined to form an anti-tank obstacle:

Massive blocks of concrete only if (1) firmly anchored to the ground by means of monolithic foundations at least two feet deep, or (2) permitted restricted movement during which they will absorb the momentum of the tank.

Rails set vertically in the ground have not proved satisfactory. Vertical rails are of the greatest value when interspersed amongst small concrete blocks or bent rails with a view to piercing the belly of the tank which falls on to them.

Bent rails (known in the Home Guard as "Hair Pins") better resist the impact of tanks. They tend to give and provide an incline which raises the front of the tank. Bent rails should be used in at least two rows at 4 foot spacing, with those in one row covering the gaps in the other. The rails should be placed with the sloping portion towards the enemy so as to lift up the front of the tank when it charges them. The height of the top of the bent rail should not be less than 2 feet 3 inches.

Horizontal rails can be laid across roads which must be kept open to traffic and are particularly effective in narrow defiles, such as between houses. At least 90-lb. rails should be used in each 13 feet of width. The height of the lowest rails above the road should be about 2 feet 6 inches and that of the top rails 4 feet 6 inches. The rails must be firmly fixed in the reinforced sides of houses or in strong concrete blocks on each side of the road and some form of keeper must be provided to prevent the rails from being jolted out of their housings.

Cables of not less than 2½ inch circumference (these will stop a 22 ton tank) can be used provided suitable anchorages are available. The cables should be suspended at the right height to catch the turret of the tank and as the tank moves forward raise the front of it off the ground. Proper anchorages include trees of not less than 2 feet in diameter. In order to catch tanks of various sizes it is necessary to have two cables at different heights.

Ditches to stop tanks must be about 18 feet wide at the top and at least 6 feet wide at the bottom. They must be nearly verticle on the face to be approached by the enemy, the other side can slope up to obtain the necessary width. The face opposed to the enemy will in most soils require revetment. In disposing of the spoil from the ditch the following points must be remembered:

1. The spoil must not assist a tank to jump the ditch by providing a favorable takeoff;

2. The tank must be prevented, so far as possible, from bringing its armament to bear on the verticle face of the ditch; and
3. The spoil must not provide cover for the enemy by obscuring the defenders' observation or field of fire.

In front of such main elements of the obstruction as have just been described the following type of smaller obstacles can be used to advantage to slow up the momentum of the tank before reaching the main obstruction:

Concrete cylinders, diameter about 2 feet, height 2 feet 6 inches. The cylinders should be spaced irregularly at about 5 feet centers in 5 rows, with bricks, curb stones or other non-rolling objects scattered on the ground amongst them.

Buoys (known to the Home Guard as "dollies"). These are reinforced concrete in the form of truncated cones with rounded bottoms. As their colloquial name "dollies" indicates they roll around on their rounded bottoms but always bob up again in the way of the tank. Their dimensions are roughly as follows: Maximum diameter 2 feet 8 inches, diameter at top 9 inches, height of truncated cone 2 feet, depth of rounded bottom 9 inches. These buoys should be spaced at about 5 foot centers in 5 rows.

Pimples are reinforced concrete blocks in the form of truncated pyramids 2 feet high on a 3 foot square base which is 1 foot deep. The top of the pimple is 1 foot square. For use in very soft ground or on beaches the base should be increased to 4 feet square. They should be spaced in 5 rows at 7 feet 6 inch centers and let into the ground 1 foot.

Coffins are sloping oblong reinforced concrete blocks. They are 1 foot 3 inches high at the lowest point and 4 to 6 feet long, rising to 2 feet 6 inches or 3 feet 6 inches in rear. They are let into the ground 1 foot. They should be about 3 feet wide and spread 4 or 5 feet apart. They should not be employed where a tank can manoeuvre to attack them obliquely.

As has been stated above the road block should be designed so that tanks cannot leave the road and bypass the block. The natural obstacles on the enemy side of the block, if not sufficient, can be reinforced by the use of anti-tank mines.

The following are some of the forms of attack and the weapons to be used against a tank once it is stopped by the obstacles of the block:

In order to keep the tank closed up, small arms fire, grenades, etc.

Driver's, Gunner's and Commander's slits subjected to: small arms fire from ground level at short range; flame; incendiary and high explosive grenades—in order to reduce the tank's visibility and ventilation and to demoralize the crew.

Louvres or air vents subject to incendiary bombing from above so that the liquid or fire will be sucked into the tank thus to upset the air intake for the engine and crew and to make it uninhabitable and possibly set it on fire.

Tracks subject to fire from anti-tank rifle (tracks of heaviest tanks have been broken by direct hits from this arm), high explosive percussion grenade, S.T. grenade, and subject to anti-tank mines, and crow-bars, picks, rails and wooden spars rammed between driving sprockets and track while moving slowly.

Belly and top of tank where there is less armor subject to anti-tank rifle fire at short range, preferably from the ground level at the belly if the tank rears up against a barrier or obstruction.

Flame used in the various ways described in weapon training. All obstacles, including road blocks, must be covered by fire. Rifles, anti-tank rifles, light machine guns and machine guns should be sited away from the block and on the flanks covering the road on the enemy side. Tank bombers should be in position on the flanks of the defile on the enemy side of the block. Snipers should be disposed to attack any enemy leaving the armored vehicle or showing himself. Some of the defending force should be disposed to prevent any out-flanking movement by the enemy. In siting fire posts and weapon pits consideration must be given to the possibility of smoke being used by the enemy to conceal their movements; it must also be remembered that although hostile armored vehicles may be expected from a certain direction, it is always possible that they may appear from the least expected quarter and consequently alternative positions must be planned and prepared to meet all situations.

In addition to the above cited instructions and official pamphlets the following official pamphlets, all of which are issued to the Home Guard, bear on the subject: Military Training Pamphlet No. 40, "Anti-Tank Mines"; "The Home Guard Can Fight"; Field Engineering Pamphlet No. 9, 1941, "Booby Traps and Tank Traps"; Infantry Training, 1937, Supplement 1941, "Tactical Notes for Platoon Commanders"; S.A.T. Vol. 1, Pamphlet No. 5, "Anti-Tank Rifles." The following unofficial publications are also used by the Home Guard in their training: "The Home Guard Training Manual," Langdon-Davies, Section V; "A Handbook for the Home Guard," Brophy; "New Ways of War," Wintringham; "Home Guard for Victory," Slater; "Hints for the Home Guard," Fitzwilliams; "How to Fight," Pilling; "Home Guard Pocketbook," Green.

The training of the Home Guard in the manning of obstacles and road blocks has been by lectures, assigned reading, by the basic training in the use of arms and by tactical exercises in which the regular army has often cooperated by acting as the enemy. The tank corps has also contributed to this training by giving the Home Guard the opportunity of examining tanks, learning their mechanism, and seeing them in action.

Village Defence: (In England the subject of "Village Defence" is treated as a general pattern for City, Town or Village, and we accordingly in this report will treat it in the same way. Naturally there is some variation depending on local conditions but the basic principles are applicable in each case.)

Comment on Village Defence by Langdon-Davies

"An invading force will not desire to capture and occupy every village that it reaches. Its object will be to get through as soon as possible and, according to a time table, to its main objective.

But you may have to defend your village because some of the invading forces, held up from the carrying out of their complete plans, desire to use it to obtain provisions and rest.

You may also have to defend your village because the roads chosen by the invaders pass through it and therefore the job of obstructing their advance may have to be done in your village streets. For any of these reasons you must be careful to understand the principles (of village defence and street fighting).

The defences of a village may be divided into the outer defences and inner defences. Your system of road blocks should surround the village and cut off all approaches to it.

By holding your road blocks you are not only slowing up the enemy's advance, but keeping him out of the village. In making ready these outer defences you must ask yourself the following questions.

(a) Have we observer posts which can see and warn us of an attack from any direction in time to have the inner defences fully prepared?

(b) Do our road blocks make the village tank-proof or have we left any entrances (perhaps through gardens or fields) open for a surprise tank attack?

(c) Can the defenders of the outer defences send back messages without the messengers having to come under fire?

(d) Have we sufficient number of messengers who know the ground perfectly so that all our outer defences can communicate rapidly with our headquarters in the village?

(e) Have we disposed our road blocks so that if necessary the defenders may retire back into the village without being cut off by the enemy."

The above are the opening paragraphs in Section IX, "Village Defence and Street Fighting" of "The Home Guard Training Manual," by Langdon-Davies recommended by the War Office as an issue to Home Guard Commanders.

Comment on Village Defence by Wintringham

In the officially issued pamphlet "The Home Guard Can Fight," prepared by Mr. Tom Wintringham, he has this to say,—"The Prime Minister has said that we will fight in every street and every house. I would go further and state we can annihilate the German Army in our streets and houses if we know how.... There is little tradition of town warfare in regular army training, because formerly cities surrendered at once or were besieged and starved out. All that is changed now... a thorough knowledge of street tactics is essential to every member of the Home Guard. Street fighting is extremely dangerous. Casualties are very high on both sides, but those of the attacker are far higher. This is because houses provide excellent cover and demolished or half demolished buildings even better cover ... So Artillery and Aerial bombardment merely provides you with new and better positions ... Tanks are very inefficient in streets. They are easily held up or slowed down by natural barriers, road blocks ... then they are at the mercy of anti-tank grenades thrown from ... upper windows ... One machine gun properly placed can dominate a whole street for hours ... Smoke bombs are essential equipment for street fighting ... In the open street, success lies in surprise and very rapid movement, but never come out into the open if you can avoid it. Your best way of advancing along a street is inside the houses knocking holes through the party walls ... Watch out for booby traps as you enter. It is often wise to send a dog in first to set off such traps ... A great deal of street fighting is at short ranges. Therefore, the Tommy Gun is the supreme weapon for this purpose, especially indoors. Mills Bombs and revolvers are excellent. Rifles are more clumsy indoors, but useful ... do not fix bayonets..."

> NOTE: Wooden houses, villages and parts of towns and cities might through firing by the enemy, either from the ground or air, become death traps instead of having the defensive availability, spoken of above. With the amount of wooden construction existent in the U. S., village defence may be less important here.

Instructions on Village Defence

Another booklet recommended by the War Office to Home Guard Commanders is "Home Guard for Victory" by Hugh Slater, which deals in detail with this subject.

The importance of this subject as viewed by the War Office is indicated by the fact that Training Instruction No. 1, 1940, treats solely on Road Blocks and Defence of Villages.

We have shown above the relationship of Road Blocks to the Defence of a Village and have covered the subject of Road Blocks in a previous sub-section.

Instruction No. 1 states:

"The main purpose of a defended village is to produce a self-contained center of resistance which will be difficult for the enemy to capture. He will thus be kept in the open until he can be counter-attacked by forces ear-marked for the purpose."

This Instruction has the following paragraph headings: 1. Tactical layout. 2. Use of buildings. 3. Communications. 4. Maps.

Instruction No. 10 deals with the tactics of the Home Guard which are applicable to the defence of a village, which include an understanding of, and cooperation with the regular military units and civilian defence services.

Instruction No. 6 deals exclusively with the relations between the Civil Defence Services and the Home Guard.

"Home Guard Instructions," printed pamphlets and booklets authorized and recommended by the War Office, together with lectures at the War Office Schools treat defence of villages as important.

Some Principles of Village Defence

Extracted from the above we give the following principles of "Village Defence."

(1) "Ideal to aim at: an invisible defending force, locally mobile, that can refuse passage to an enemy force twice as numerous, can harry and immobilize a force four times as numerous, and cannot be stamped out by a force twenty times as numerous."

(2) "Basic conceptions of defence: the defended 'locality'; the 'tank-proof island'; the 'strong point'; the 'keep'; and the counter-attack."

(3) Intimate knowledge of locality—streets, back alley ways, gardens, etc. and how to move through them and around them in the safest way and at the proper time, using if necessary such unusual channels as subways, manholes, sewers, etc.

(4) Intimate knowledge of all buildings—how to move around, over or through them—and in the safest way. (The enemy may have occupied some of them.)

(5) Communications by private or special telephones—independent signal systems—intelligent messenger service.

(6) Proper fortifications and action stations on perimeter and within the village. "Prepare for a multiplicity of positions; many more than can be constantly manned but to be used dependent upon the direction from which the enemy comes. He may come from any direction."

(7) Knowledge of concealment and camouflage.

(8) Knowledge of weapons—the proper ones to use in the proper places.

(9) Positions for telling "lines of fire". "Be fully posted on distances and ranges in your entire locality."

(10) Knowledge of Fieldcraft—Scouting—Guiding.

NOTE: "The Home Guard Training Manual" by Langdon-Davies states:—
"Naturally there will be some units of the Home Guard stationed in places where the detailed rules laid down in this section (Fieldcraft) do not apply. For example, the Home Guard of a London suburb will not have to deal with the problems set by hedgerows and small streams. That does not mean he should omit this section (Fieldcraft) since it will help him to understand the problem of the defence of Britain as a whole."

It has also been pointed out that the city Home Guard Unit in the event of a successful attack might be driven out of the city or city suburb, at which time an understanding of Fieldcraft might easily prove invaluable.

(11) Proper and safe locations of "headquarters."

(12) Plan for special accommodations of the local Home Guard. They may be required to spend a week or more away from home.

(13) Plan to have in your platoon liaison officers who are good mixers. "A good mixer can interest the neighborhood in your activities. Neighbors can help in every way."

(14) Plan for supplies of food, clothing, etc. secretly cached—with full knowledge of all sources of water supply.

(15) Plan for demolition of food—petrol—and such supplies as might be of aid to a successful enemy.

(16) Plan for secret avenues with as much cover as possible available for arrival from the outside of reinforcements, messengers, supplies, etc., which avenues may also be used, if necessary, as avenues of escape.

(17) Plan for a rallying point—available for men who become separated—or where unsuccessful messengers can report to.

(18) Plan for the handling of casualties.

(19) Plan for control over civilian population in cooperation with police and other civilian forces.

Comment by Col. Shortt on Control of Civilians

Colonel Shortt, G.S.O.I. Military Training Home Guard (M.T.7) had this to say on the subject:

"Uncontrolled and panicky civilians . . . are a great hindrance, and the Germans with their Fifth Column activities, their spreading of limitless amounts of reports, their forcing of refugees on to the highways, and all such tactics would prove detrimental to the British movements. The duties of the Home Guard are to prove from where the information comes, sift that information and not spread any ill-found reports."

(20) Knowledge of Guerrilla Warfare.

(21) "There is a time to be brave, but ordinarily do everything to protect yourself. A man can use intelligence. A live man is better for offense and defence than a dead one. Learn all the rules of your game first before you start out trying to get shot."

(22) "Be just as ruthless with the Germans as they have been with us."

It can thus be seen that all the tactics and training of the Home Guard, to a greater or lesser extent depending on local conditions, are applicable to the defence of a village. In addition to the basic training involved and described in former paragraphs, the Home Guard have tactical exercises, time trials on manning their action stations, etc.

Anti-Aircraft Defence of a Village

The anti-aircraft defence of a "village" is the responsibility of the regular army except that, as noted in this report, certain units of the Home Guard are allotted to anti-aircraft duties under the command of the regular army.

Factory Defence

Factory Defence: From the "Defence of a Village" one steps naturally into the "Defence of a Factory," as so many of the basic principles are equally applicable in both cases.

The importance of production is emphasized from every angle. The destruction of large and vital industrial plants is one of the enemy's main objectives.

There has developed in the formation of the Home Guard, what might be called two sub-divisions.

(1) Large factories or groups of factories in one contiguous locality which have organized Home Guard Units within themselves and whose defence job is, except in special cases, confined to the factory or factory group alone.

(2) Smaller factories whose Home Guard Forces operate in co-operation with the Home Guard Forces of that locality. Sub-division No. 1 is usually of Battalion strength. Sub-division No. 2 has units consistent with the size of the factory.

Members of the Home Guard Units in both divisions are made up of the factory employers and employees. Difficulty has been encountered where employers have not joined in with the employees in establishing a proper balance between "time devoted to production" and "time devoted to Home Guard duties."

"Factory Units"
(Memorandum by Capt. E. H. Ryley)

From an early memorandum prepared by Captain E. H. Ryley, Deputy Assistant Director, Home Guard Directorate, we present the following data:

"At the start, the number of strictly factory units formed was very large, undoubtedly because the defense of a factory appealed strongly both to employer and employee. This caused in many instances considerable waste of manpower arising from the fact that a very large number of Home Guards were engaged in purely static tasks. Furthermore in some districts the local Home Guard Commanders being conscious of the waste of manpower, developed a distinct antagonism to the factory units in their areas and gave them little assistance in obtaining equipment or in training.

It became necessary therefore for the War Office to lay down the general policy to be followed with regard to these Factory Units and this was done early in August 1940. Factories are divided into two categories:

(1) Factories placed on a priority list by the Ministry of Home Security by reason of their substantial national importance.

(2) All other factories.

Those in Category (1) were given preference in obtaining arms and equipment and special arrangements were made to insure that the training of members of these units should not interfere with their work. So far as those in Category (2) were concerned, while the formation of Factory Units of such places was permitted, it was not encouraged and the persons concerned were informed that better service would be rendered by joining a regular local Home Guard Unit."

Official Instructions on Factory Defence

Instructions Nos. 2, 4 and 10 deal broadly with this subject of Factory Defense, but Instruction No. 12, 1940, exclusively with this subject. It states—

"The object will be to guard against:
    (1) Sabotage
    (2) Espionage
    (3) Ground Attack
    (4) Air Attack

It further states—"In any defence scheme the tasks of the Home Guard, A.R.P. and fire-fighting services must be carefully coordinated ... Reliable and suitable communications should be arranged with the local military authorities and the local Home Guard Commander," and emphasizes as well that "The defence scheme should cater for the security of the factory by day and night." This Instruction deals in some detail with the above four subjects.

The subject of "Defence of a Factory" is included in the curriculum of the War Office Schools and is covered in various memoranda prepared by Home Guard Commanders who have already formed "Factory Units."

Certain unofficial publications recommended by the War Office, such as "Home Guard for Victory" by Hugh Slater, deal with this subject.

> NOTE: The above "Instructions" and pamphlets will be available as exhibits in our Main Report.

General Role of Home Guard as Applied to Factory Defence

In addition to preparing against the rather special dangers of sabotage and espionage, such basic training of the Home Guard is applicable to Factory Defense as:
    Siting and designing of posts
    Concealment and camouflage
    Cover from view
    Cover from fire

Organization, duties, training and weapons are in the main similar to those of the regular Home Guard Units, but with certain special exceptions; such as the direction over employees when the factory is being evacuated during an air raid, and the subsequent cooperation with the A.R.P. Forces in the Factory Air Raid Shelters.

We had the opportunity of visiting several factories and noted the cooperation with the regular military forces in such factories as were working on important defense products. This included anti-air-craft defense.

Control of Employees in Factory Defence

We noted also the special factory "Map" or "Control" rooms, which were connected directly or indirectly with regional or military report centers. It was from these special rooms that "call for duty" signals were given Factory Units and special warnings were sounded for the evacuation of the factory in event of an air raid. The employees of such factories were instructed not to act on the public "alert." As one of the Factory Unit Commanders said to us—"It places a grave responsibility on our shoulders in waiting until the last minute before ordering the evacuation of our group of factories in the interests of keeping up production."

Instruction No. 12 contains a very helpful appendix headed:

"Points to be remembered in preparing a Factory Scheme of Defence."

Points to be Remembered in Preparing a Factory Scheme of Defence

1. The system of checking entry into the factory—
    (a) Passes for employees.
    (b) Rules for admission for visitors.
    (c) Written orders for gate detachments to include:
        i. methods of challenging by day and night;
        ii. orders for the disposal of visitors;
        iii. action in the case of suspicious visitors.
2. Observation posts
    (a) Number required.
    (b) Strength of each post.
    (c) Written orders for each post to include:
        i. part of perimeter and vital points for which responsible;
        ii. means of communication;
        iii. action to be taken if suspicions aroused.
3. Patrols
    (a) Numbers required, by day, by night.
    (b) Responsibility for instructions as to route and time.
4. Entries
    (a) Which are to be permanently blocked.
    (b) What others have to be blocked? When is this to be done? Who gives the order? Is material available at hand? Are detachments detailed?
5. Weapons
    (a) Number available of different types.
    (b) Distribution to cover approaches to best advantage.
    (c) Does number available permit of a reserve?
6. Defense posts
    (a) Number required.
    (b) Are they concealed and protected from ground and air attack? Are detachments detailed?
    (c) Written orders for each post to include:
        i. Number of men.
        ii. Number of weapons.
        iii. Limits of perimeter for which responsible.
        iv. Range cards.
        v. S.A.A. to be held in post.
        vi. Care and cleaning of weapons.
        vii. Communications with defense H.Q.

7. Reserves
    (a) Location.
    (b) Strength and organization in parties.
    (c) Is there moderate comfort for them?
    (d) Reserves of S.A.A. where held.
8. System of reliefs
9. The Alarm signal
    (a) What is it?
    (b) Who is authorized to give it?
    (c) Does everybody know what to do?
10. Communications
    (a) From Defense H.Q. to posts, and to H.Q. of the military commander;
    (b) from post to post;
    (c) arrangements for keeping roads and alleys clear.
11. Defense H.Q.
    (a) Location, liaison with A.R.P. H.Q.
    (b) Arrangements for protection.
12. Administrative arrangements
    (a) Casualties.
    (b) Tools.
    (c) Blankets, waterproof sheets.
    (d) Food, water.
    (e) Latrines.
13. Anti-gas measures
14. Liaison
    (a) with local military commander;
    (b) with outside Home Guard commanders;
    (c) with police;
    (d) with civil authorities.
15. Suitable times for rehearsal and practice.

As stated above much of the training is in the basic fundamentals, but exercises in manning the action stations and in defense tactics, are also employed.

Guerrilla Warfare

Guerrilla Warfare: In the officially issued pamphlet, "The Home Guard Can Fight," there appears in the introduction—"... a guerrilla fights in an area that the enemy thinks he has occupied—an area from which the guerrilla's own regular forces have withdrawn or in which they have been killed off."

Langdon-Davies says in his "Home Guard Training Manual": "Once you are called into action the chance is ten to one that you will be isolated, and have to make your own decision. The more you know, the more you will be able to harass the enemy."

It naturally follows that to be effective in Guerrilla Warfare the guerrilla (individually or in small units) must be versed in the subject. Instruction No. 14 contains this statement:

"It is of the greatest importance that every Home Guard Unit and sub-unit should have no doubts about the role allotted to it. The standard of training should aim at preparing the unit to carry out that role ... training in guerrilla warfare ... may be an important part of the tactics of the defence of a locality."

The following publications recommended by the War Office touch on this subject: "Home Guard Training Manual" by Langdon-Davies; "Home Guard for Victory" by Hugh Slater; "New Ways of War" by Wintringham.

The War Office Schools and instructors to the Home Guard emphasize the importance of "Guerrilla Warfare."

Guerrilla Warfare (By Lectures and Pamphlets, etc.)

Guerrilla Warfare: (a) By Lectures, Pamphlets, etc.

1. Plan for a definite place or places to gather in rendezvous if and when the Home Guard has been scattered as a result of a successful enemy action in any locality. Arrange for a "hoped for" temporary headquarters where emergency supplies have been secretly cached and from which place guerrilla warfare can be initiated. "Have changes of clothes and weapons hidden around in different spots in your neighborhood."
2. Know every inch of your locality—within houses and towns—streets—back alley ways—and surrounding country. "The enemy does not know the local territory—the Home Guard does. Act accordingly."
3. Know local population.
4. Knowledge of Fieldcraft—Scouting—Guiding.
5. Knowledge of Camouflage.
6. Knowledge of decontamination.
7. Knowledge of small arms—what can be used and how and when to use them—such as "sniping."
   Training Instructions No. 8, 1940, contains this paragraph: "Darkness is the greatest ally of the tank hunter. As night approaches the tanks seek harbors where they may lie up and rest. This is the opportunity for stalking, sniping, and attacking with grenades and incendiary bombs. On no account must they be allowed to rest undisturbed."
8. Improvised weapons, where to carry them—how to use them—and what they will accomplish—such as daggers—hatpins—hammers—hose pipes, etc.
9. Booby traps—traps in great variety that will hurt or scare the enemy. Emphasis on individual ingenuity. (See Field Engineering Pamphlet No. 9, 1941 "Booby Traps and Tank Traps"). Schemes for the use of Automatic Explosives can be worked up through ingenuity. In fact, things unheard of with elements of surprise count a lot."
10. How to capture and handle individuals or small groups of the enemy such as sentries—messengers, etc.

11. Improvised tank—car—and motorcycle blocks.

"Quick action for a surprise road block is to take first (a few feet above the ground), the bark off a tree. Then saw the tree to a point just before it is ready to fall. Nail the bark back over the cut section of the tree so that it will look natural. Attach a rope or wire to the top of the tree and carry it to an appropriate station on the side of the road. Wait for an automobile that you believe contains officers. This may be determined by some scout and communicated by some prearranged signal from a point further down the road. At the proper signal pull the tree over. It will block the road and the car will come to a stop. Then bomb the officers in the car."

12. Know how to move individually and in groups with correct system of signals.
13. Have appreciation of elements of surprise.
14. Elements of "ambush."
15. Identification of German Units (See Pocket Notes on Identification of German Units, July, 1940).
16. Knowledge of common German Military Expressions (See Instruction No. 15, 1940).

Guerilla Warfare (By Exercises)

Guerilla Warfare: (b) By Exercises.
1. Hunting out "the enemy" in a woods.
2. Locating and "tracking" the enemy by night.
3. Practice tests in camouflage.

NOTE: There are many practical exercises that demonstrate the keenness of the senses and the ingenuity of the enemy and the Home Guard. Exercises in Fieldcraft, Scouting and Guerrilla Tactics are closely related.

Guides

Guides: In an interview with General Sir Alan Brooke, Commander-in-Chief of all the Forces in the British Isles, he said: "One of the very important functions of the Home Guard will be that of acting in the capacity of guides for the 'Regular' Forces. Their intimate knowledge of their locality makes their services of inestimable value."

In Training Instruction No. 2, 1940 issued in June (less than a month after the Home Guard was formed), first mention is made of "Guides" as follows:

"Volunteers (Home Guard) with local knowledge will be of value in guiding military parties both across country and on roads. (The last task is of added importance now that sign-posts have been removed.)"

The subject of "Guides" is again referred to in Instruction No. 10, 1940, headed "General Instructions." This was issued on August 1st, 1940 and contains the following paragraph:

"Home Guards may legitimately be called upon to act as guides to military parties proceeding by road or across country by day or night. In this role they are likely to be particularly valuable now that all sign-posts and means of identification have been removed."

In Instruction No. 14, 1940 the subject of "Guides" was included in "Winter Training."

It is very apparent that in the steadily broadening "role" of the Home Guard greater and greater responsibilities were placed on the shoulders of members of the Home Guard who had been assigned the task of acting as guides. This led up to the issue in December, 1940 of Instruction No. 22 devoted entirely to that subject.

Referring to the fact that the Home Guard "may be required to act as guides to the Field Army" this instruction in the main, states:

(1) "Training will now take place to develop in the Home Guard an organization which will enable commanders of formations and units to get full value from those having special knowledge."

(2) "It is suggested that the organization should consist of a chief guide appointed for a specified area with guides on a general basis of one per parish, with understudies..."

(3) "The object ... to provide readily accessible sources of local intelligence..."

(4) "Instruction should be organized under the following headings:
   a. Geographical and topographical knowledge.
   b. General local knowledge.
   c. Local military knowledge.

(5) Subject "a" is developed under sub-headings of a very detailed nature such as—
   (1) Routes and distances.
   (2) Road classification.
   (3) Rivers and streams.
   (4) Knowledge of tracks, fords, ferries, etc.
   (5) Railways.
   (6) Bridges.
   (7) Local vegetation.

(6) Subject "b" is developed in detail requiring knowledge of "Positions" of all types of public service buildings, etc.—complete information on all "Local telephone systems"—"Local electricity supply" and "Local water supply."

(7) Subject "c" requires knowledge of the "best observation posts" properly mapped. Knowledge of "suitable camp sites" and "covered harborage for vehicles." Knowledge of railway "accommodations" and "covered storage." Local information which "with the aid of a Regular officer ... is likely to be of use in laying out the tactical defence of the area."

It can be readily seen from the above that the task allotted to Home Guard Guides is included ordinarily in "Military Intelligence" and this places grave responsibilities on the shoulders of Home Guard Commanders and Instructors.

Accordingly to meet the specified requirements it is obvious that Guides must, among other things, have full knowledge of "Fieldcraft," "Concealment and Camouflage" and Home Guard tactics in general.

Instructions for "Guides" and all the above related subjects are given at the War Office Schools for Home Guard Instructors. Thus complete instruction in this subject is available.

Special Jobs

Special Jobs: Because of their local character several jobs which are similar to the peace time functions of our National Guard are included in the mission of the Home Guard. It is contemplated that, in cases of emergency such as an unusually severe bombing of a city, the Home Guard will co-operate with the Civil Defence Forces. The Regional Commissioners or other Civil Defence Authorities cannot, however, order the Home Guard into such action. These authorities request co-operation from the local military commander (Home Guard or regular army, whichever it may be), who issues the orders to the Home Guard. The reason, of course, is that the military commander, responsible for the military defence of the area, must have the say as to whether the troops can be spared for such non-military purposes. The Home Guard in London and other cities have rendered yeoman service in co-operation with the Civil Defence Forces during severe "blitz." Instruction No. 10 includes in the functions of the Home Guard "Co-operation with the Civil Defence Services," and it specifically mentions "fire-fighting, particularly crops and woods in rural areas." Our impression is that there have been few fires of this latter type (in our country with our great areas of wild forest and the dryness of some of our crop areas, this might be very different). The training of the Home Guard has as yet included little specialized training in fire-fighting or other Civil Defence subjects, probably because they have been so busy training for their primary job of military defence.

Control of Civilian Population

Control of Civilian Population: Mention has been made before in this report of the use made by the Germans of the masses of refugees on the roads of Belgium and France. In Great Britain today, unless it has been evacuated prior to the start of active operations, the civilian population is to "stay put" and only move on the orders of the military command. It is contemplated that under certain conditions local movements may be ordered, and it will be the job of the Home Guard to see that these movements are orderly and made on unused roads, etc. so as not to interfere with military movements. It is also felt that the Home Guard will be a great assistance in keeping the local population from being the means of spreading false or exaggerated rumors, from panicking, and moving without orders. (See statements made to us by Lt. Gen. T. R. Eastwood (Page 16 of this report) and Col. Ebenezer Pike (Page 16). Instruction No. 4 spoke of "assistance to police in control of civil population" as one of the "tasks" of the Home Guard. This was carried over into the directive, Instruction No. 10, but in this case it is not described as "assistance to police." It has become a direct duty of the Home Guard. The only form of training which might be said to specifically belong to this task is the forming of cordons (rather similar to some of our riot training). Instruction No. 5, in speaking of training for this job, says: "This should be practiced, ranks extending rapidly to a flank, each man keeping his proper place and the extension which is ordered."

Due to the predominence of wooden construction in parts of the U. S. it seems necessary here to plan for the evacuation of large sections of the civilian population in case of invasion or even bombing from the air. In these movements of the population such a force as the Home Guard might be very useful.

Bomb Reconnaissance

Bomb Reconnaissance: Instruction No. 26 provides as follows: "It should be especially noted that while reconnaissance and reporting of unexploded bombs is a duty of the Home Guard, bomb disposal is not a commitment of the force. All unexploded bombs, except the small 1 kilogram incendiary bombs, and all unexploded parachute mines, must be reported immediately to the police."

In this connection Military Training Pamphlet No. 45, 1941, "Bomb Reconnaissance and Protection Against Unexploded Bombs (All Arms)" has been distributed to the Home Guard. This training pamphlet gives directions for training military units in locating unexploded bombs and taking the necessary safety precautions pending the arrival of bomb disposal parties. It also places on the Home Guard the duty of removing from their own area to some suitable place designated by their commander, small, unignited incendiary bombs, unexploded aeroplane cannon shells and unexploded anti-aircraft shells. It provides for prompt reporting of all such bombs and shells when located.

NOTE: Bomb Reconnaissance is the task of all civilians under the direction of the Regional Commissioner as well as the military.

PART THREE—LAW AND ORGANIZATION

Section F. Authority

SECTION F—*Authority for the Home Guard.*

NOTE: In reference to the various subjects under Part Three we desire to call attention to the fact that these same subjects will be covered in detail in our Main Report with the official papers attached as exhibits.

The basic enabling legislation is the Emergency Power (Defence) Act of 1939 passed by Parliament on 24 August 1939. This act gave the Ministry the right and power to do almost anything necessary for the defence of the country.

Under this Act the Home Guard was formed by "The Defence (Local Defence Volunteers) Regulations 1940." By this the establishment and control of the Force was placed in the Army Council.

Under this authority the Army Council issues from time to time Army Council Instructions (A.C.Is.) Orders, etc., governing the Home Guard.

Section G. Legal Status of Members

SECTION G—*Legal Status of Members of the Home Guard*

At International Law

At International Law

By The Defence (Local Defence Volunteers) Regulations 1940 the members of the Home Guard are members of the armed forces of the Crown. Consequently they have all the rights and powers given to the armed forces of a belligerent by the laws of war. They may oppose the enemy by all methods and means not specifically forbidden by International Law. They in turn may be killed or wounded by the enemy just so long as they continue to fight, but when they surrender they are entitled to be treated as prisoners of war.

At Military Law

At Military Law

The regulations establishing the Home Guard subject the members of this Force to The Army Act. This Act is the basic enactment of British Military Law, consequently the members of the Force are subject to the punishments for military offences mentioned in The Army Act. These offences are the usual military offences such as abandoning a post, casting away arms, ammunition, etc., giving intelligence to the enemy, harboring the enemy, showing or inducing cowardice, plundering, drunkenness, mutiny, sedition, insubordination to superior officers, disobeying orders, deserting, etc.

At Civil Law

At Civil Law

In Great Britain at Common Law a person by becoming a member of the armed forces and therefore submitting himself to military law does not relieve himself of all his civil obligations. His civilian status is modified but he retains many rights and liabilities.

The Army Act specifically provides that a soldier shall not be taken out of His Majesty's forces except on account of a charge of or conviction for a crime or on account of any debt, damage or sum of money which exceeds £30.

Though a member of the Home Guard is criminally liable he is excused if he was acting under orders and if he reasonably could assume that the orders were proper, thus a sentry is not liable for shooting a person who ignores his challenge or for firing on looters if ordered to do so by his commander.

A member of the Home Guard under certain conditions is liable for work done for the Home Guard, namely, if he did not have proper authority to order the work. Under certain conditions a member of the Home Guard is also liable for damages for negligence, trespass, etc.

Powers, Rights and Duties Under Certain Acts

Powers, Rights and Duties under Certain Acts

Certain rights of interference with the normal rights of citizens are conferred on members of the Home Guard by The Defence (General) Regulations 1939 as Amended. Under these regulations it is made the duty of the armed forces of the Crown to enforce them and the Home Guard are consequently given the power to do so. These regulations provide for most of the war time control over the property and citizens of England. A member of the Home Guard must neither use his powers wantonly nor fail to use them when the occasion arises.

Under these regulations a member of the Home Guard may arrest without warrant on reasonable grounds for suspicion that the person arrested is committing or about to commit an offence against the regulations. These offences include various acts such as giving information to the enemy, interfering with essential services, improperly using wireless, improperly taking photographs, entering prohibited places, harboring prisoners, looting, publishing false reports, and many others.

A member of the Home Guard can question anyone and detain them for twenty-four hours, but must then turn them over to the police, or, if he obtains police approval, he can detain them for a period up to seven days.

He can stop anyone and ask them for their identity card.

A member of the Home Guard has no right to search premises on his own authority, but he may be authorized to do so by a Justice of the Peace, or in case of urgency, by a police officer of rank not lower than Superintendent.

By a general provision of the Regulations he may use such force as is reasonably necessary for the purpose of exercising his rights and powers, for instance, if he is refused entry he may break open the door.

He may stop and search automobiles, other vehicles and vessels.

If any unattended automobile is not rendered incapable of being driven away, he may render it so.

He may enforce the black-out.

He may enforce the regulations for the control of gasoline, and may enter and inspect premises to enforce such regulations.

He can reconnoiter without committing trespass.

He has a right to enter land and to dig trenches weapon pits, defence posts, etc., and to put up such obstructions as anti-tank traps and obstructions against the landing of enemy aircraft.

Members of the Home Guard who wish to take possession of land, house or buildings must apply to their immediate Home Guard Commander who in turn applies to his immediate regular Army Commander, the latter obtains the proper authority. The same is true for the requisitioning of personal property, such as automobiles, motorcycles, etc.

By the National Service (Armed Forces) Act 1939 and The National Service (Armed Forces) (Prevention of Invasion) Regulations 1939 and 1940 a member of the Home Guard is protected from being discharged from his employment because of any duties which he has had to perform in connection with the Home Guard.

By The Motor Vehicles (Variation of Speed Limit) Provisional Regulations, 1940, a member of the Home Guard when driving an automobile for military purposes and subject to orders from a superior officer is subject to no speed limit.

By the Military Service (Armed Forces) Act, 1940, membership in the Home Guard does not exempt the member from being "called up" for compulsory military service.

Section H. Organization

Army Council

SECTION H—*Organization*.

As appeared above the organization and control of the Home Guard was vested in the Army Council. In compliance with this authority the Army Council from time to time issues instructions known as "A.C.Is", orders, regulations, etc.

War Office

The members of the Army Council cannot personally conduct the vast business of running the Crown Forces. They must delegate much of their work. The group which does their work is known collectively as "The War Office." By A.C.I. No. 924 of 1940 all the controls, except the operational command of the Home Guard, are the responsibility of the War Office. Consequently, various controls of the Home Guard run through various members of the War Office and their departments.

Chain of Command "Regular" Forces

As stated before in this report the operational command and certain administrative controls are tied in closely with the regular army organization. In order to give the background necessary to understand the situation the three main chains of command of the regular army will here be described. These three main chains of command are (1) for the mobile forces, (2) for the static troops other than Anti-Aircraft, and (3) for the Anti-Aircraft troops.

(1) The chain of command for the mobile forces of the regular army runs from the Commander-in-Chief, Home Forces, through the army commands, corps, divisions, brigades, battalions, companies, platoons to the sections.

(2) The chain of command for the static troops of the regular army, other than Anti-Aircraft, runs from the Commander-in-Chief, Home Forces, through the army commands, areas, sub-areas, to the special units of the regular army which are static, such as training centers, depots, etc.

(3) The chain of command for the anti-aircraft troops of the regular army runs from the General Officer, Commanding-in-Chief, Anti-Aircraft Command, through the anti-aircraft divisions, anti-aircraft battalions, anti-aircraft companies, anti-aircraft batteries, to the anti-aircraft sections.

Home Guard Units and Their Commanders

Home Guard Units and Their Commanders

Authority for the formation of units of the Home Guard must be obtained from the Home Guard Directorate. The Home Guard is organized within the military areas. In each military area a Home Guard Area Commander may be appointed. Each Military Area includes one or more Home Guard Zones, each under a Zone Commander. Each Zone may be formed into two or more Home Guard Groups, each Group under a Group Commander. Each Zone or Group is made up of two or more Battalions. Each Battalion is sub-divided into Companies, Companies into Platoons, and Platoons into Sections. The normal basis is four companies to a battalion, four platoons to a company, and four sections to a platoon, each unit under its own commander.

Certain Government Departments, railway companies, public utility undertakings and factories are permitted to form Home Guard Units in which their employees are enrolled primarily for the protection of their undertakings. These units normally form sub-units of the local Home Guard battalion, group or zone, and their employment on their special tasks are coordinated with the Local Defence scheme by the military commander concerned.

Local tactical necessity and the available personnel determines the number of units in each case.

Chains of Operational Command Home Guard

Chains of Operational Command of The Home Guard

For all Home Guard Units, other than those allotted to Anti-Aircraft Units, the chain of operational command passes from the Commander-in-Chief, Home Forces, through the Army Commands, the Areas, Sub-Areas and the regular army officers commanding the regular army sub-units to which the Home Guard sub-units are attached.

For all Home Guard Units allotted to Anti-Aircraft duties, the chain of operational command passes from the General Officer, Commanding-in-Chief Anti-Aircraft, through the Anti-Aircraft Divisions, Anti-Aircraft Battalions, Anti-Aircraft Companies to whatever sub-units of the Regular Anti-Aircraft troops the sub-units of the Home Guard are attached.

These chains of operational command reveal that, because the Home Guard must necessarily cooperate so closely with the regular troops, there is no real Home Guard chain of operational command. The chains are those of the regular army until and unless there is no regular army chain to be utilized. If lower units of the Home Guard than the Battalion are not attached to regular army units, there may be a truly Home Guard chain of command from the Battalion to the lower unit, but for operational purposes the Home Guard chain never extends higher than the Battalion Commander.

Chain of Control for Training Purposes

Control for Training

Though the Commander-in-Chief, Home Forces, is responsible for the training of the Home Guard other than those units allotted to Anti-Aircraft, he is under the direction of the Director of Military Training of the War Office. Though the General Officer, Commanding-in-Chief Anti-Aircraft Command, is responsible for the training of those units of the Home Guard which are attached to the regular Anti-Aircraft troops, he is under the direction of the Director of Anti-Aircraft and Coast Defence of the War Office. The training of the troops is, as a matter of practice, initiated and controlled by these two Directors and their Directorates. Otherwise, the chain of control for training in both cases follows exactly the chain of operational command.

Chain of Control for Administration and Supply of The Home Guard

Control for Administration and Supply Home Guard

The supply of rations is initiated by the Director of Supplies and Transport of the War Office as is that for the regular army. His regular service handles the rations usually until delivery to the Home Guard Battalion or even Company, depending upon circumstances.

For certain specified purposes the chain of administrative control passes from the Director General, Home Guard, or the Director of Staff Duties and Director of Ordnance Services, all of the War Office, through the Territorial Associations to the Zone, or Home Guard Battalion, depending on the circumstances. These purposes are:

  a. Accommodation.
  b. Allowance and Expenses.
  c. Clothing, Equipment and Stores (including ordnance).
  d. Compensation and Claims.
  e. Finance and Accounts.
  f. Records of Personnel.
  g. Transport.

All the remaining administrative matters originate with the Director General, Home Guard, and pass through the Army Commands and Areas to the Home Guard Zones and thus through the regular Home Guard chain which may include a Group, finally to the Home Guard section.

Tables of Organization (The British use the word "Establishment")

Tables of Organization

There is no fixed table of organization, either for the make-up of the units or the number of sub-units in a higher unit. The size of Zone, Group, and Battalion Headquarters depends on the local requirements and the volume of work to be handled. This flexibility of organization is maintained so that the units can be organized to meet the particular tactical necessity of each locality.

Home Guard Officers—Assignments and Rank: The rank of the officers assigned to the higher commands is as follows:

Home Guard

Home Guard Area Commander—Brigadier

Rank

Zone Commander—Colonel
Group Commander—Colonel

Staff Officers: Staff Officers in the British Army are divided into three branches, General (G), Adjutant General's (A) and Quarter-Master General's (Q). Sometimes the duties of the two latter are combined in one officer. The Home Guard Staffs vary greatly. Normally they might be said to run as follows: Zone or Group Commander's Staff; Second in Command—Lieutenant Colonel; Staff Officer G—Major; Staff Officer A/Q—Captain.

Line Officers: The rank of the officers assigned to Line duty is as follows:

Battalion Commander—Lieutenant Colonel
Battalion Second in Command—Major
Company Commander—Major
Company Second in Command—Captain
Platoon Commander—First Lieutenant
Platoon Officer (Section Commander, etc.)—Second Lieutenant

An officer with the rank of Major is appointed to each Home Guard Battalion to act as Medical Officer.

Appointive Authority

Officers—Appointive Authority: The General Officer, Commanding-in-Chief of the Army Command appoints and promotes up to and including rank of Major. The War Office appoints and promotes the ranks of Brigadier, Colonel and Lieutenant Colonel on the nomination of the General Officer, Commanding-in-Chief of the Army Command.

Precedence

Officers—Precedence: The precedence of officers of the Home Guard is determined by their rank and the date of appointment to that rank. When serving with members of the regular forces officers of the Home Guard take precedence below regular officers of corresponding rank. An officer of the Home Guard does not automatically take command of those junior to him in the regular army, but he does so only on orders from the superior regular commander.

Qualifications

Officers—Qualifications: Officers must normally be British subjects whose fathers were natural born or naturalized British subjects, except that in special cases subjects of allied or neutral states may be commissioned by War Office authority.

Age limits between 17 and 65.

No one who refused military service in the last war can be commissioned.

Enrollment in the Home Guard is a condition precedent to being commissioned in the Home Guard.

No medical standard is laid down but officers must have a sufficient degree of mental and physical fitness to do their jobs.

Officers are chosen primarily for their powers of leadership and the confidence which they are likely to inspire in all ranks.

Home Guard Commissions

Home Guard Commissions: All officers in the Home Guard are granted a King's Commission under "The Home Guard Officers' Commissions Order, 1941."

The British, in a mistaken idea that it was necessary to eliminate all rank from the Force in order to create a body with the essential characteristics of a "Citizen Force" and "organized on the principles of equality of service and status," attempted to have no commissioned officers when the Home Guard was organized. This they found to be a mistake and have since corrected.

Any other form of regular commission held by officers appointed to the Home Guard is regarded as being held in abeyance so long as they retain their commissions in the Home Guard.

Essential Differences

Essential Differences between Home Guard Commissions and Others: Home Guard Officers do not have the right (1) to complain to the Army Council for redress of wrongs, and (2) to summarily punish one charged with an offence against military law either in their own immediate command or on reference (see "Discipline," below).

Continuity of Home Guard Commissions

Continuity of Home Guard Commission: In the Home Guard the Commission goes with the job. When an officer is relieved or resigns from his command his commission terminates, but he still remains a member of the Home Guard unless he complies with the provisions for resignation from that force or his connection therewith is terminated by competent authority.

Resignations and Terminations

Home Guard Officers—Resignations and Terminations of Appointment: Officers are normally required to give three months' notice to voluntarily terminate their appointment. An officer is subject to the same disciplinary procedure as any other member of the force. Consequently he can be discharged by competent authority for cause.

Home Guard Warrant Officers and N.C.Os.

Home Guard Warrant Officers and N.C.Os.: There are no fixed tables of organization for Warrant Officers and N.C.Os. in the different units. The numbers depend in each case on local requirements.

The following table is not in normal circumstances exceeded:

For each Battalion Headquarters:
    1 Warrant Officer, Class I (Regimental Sergeant-major)
    1 Warrant Officer, Class II (Regimental Quartermaster-Sergeant)
    1 Color Sergeant (Orderly-room Sergeant)
    4 Sergeants
    4 Corporals

For each Company Headquarters:
    1 Warrant Officer, Class II (Company Sergeant-major)
    1 Color Sergeant (Company Quartermaster-Sergeant)
    1 Corporal

For each Platoon Headquarters:
1 Sergeant
1 Corporal

For each Section Headquarters:
1 Sergeant
1 Corporal

In each Squad (subdivisions of sections where necessary):
1 Corporal

Lance-Corporals (equivalent to our Privates-First Class) may be appointed on a scale of one to each ten Privates.

Appointive Authority

Appointive Authority: Appointments to Warrant Officer Class I are made by the Zone Commander. Appointments to Sergeant and Warrant Officer Class II are made by the Battalion Commander. Appointments to N.C.O. rank below Sergeant are made by Company Commander. The same authority may for cause order reversion to a lower rank.

Resignations and Terminations

Resignations and Terminations of Appointment: Warrant Officers and N.C.Os. may resign by 14 days' notice in writing. They are subject to the same disciplinary procedure as any other member of the force, consequently they can be discharged by competent authority for cause.

Enrollment of Members of the Home Guard

Enrollment of Members of the Home Guard: To enroll in the Home Guard a man must be between the ages of 17 and 65, must be of reasonable physical fitness, and must be either (1) a British subject, or (2) a national by birth of an allied or neutral state, but neither a British subject nor a national of an allied or neutral state is eligible if he also possesses German, Austrian or Italian nationality, unless the applicant served with the British Forces in the last War. Also a national of an allied or neutral state is not eligible if he is married to a woman of German, Austrian or Italian birth unless he served with the British Forces in the last War.

Conditions of Enrollment

Conditions of Enrollment: Members of the Home Guard cannot be required (1) to give whole time service, (2) to live away from their homes, or (3) to enroll for a period exceeding the period of the present emergency. The service of a member may be determined by competent authority for cause at any time or he may resign by giving 14 days' notice in writing. Usually no objection is raised to an enrollment for a shorter period than the duration if there is some good reason. There is no ban whatever to reenrollment after voluntary resignation.

Enrollment does not exempt members from liability to register and to be "called up" for compulsory military service.

Enrollment subjects the member of the Home Guard to military law as a soldier.

Enrollment Procedure

Enrollment Procedure: Applicants register at their local police station. The Company Commander selects with the recommendation of the police from the list of applicants maintained by the local police authority those whom he wishes to enroll.

Enrollment Extensions

Enrollment Extensions: In exceptional cases members of the Home Guard are continued beyond the age of 65 years if they are both mentally and physically fit to carry out their duties and if retention is to the advantage of the unit.

Transfers

Transfers: When a member of the Home Guard moves and wishes to transfer to a new unit he first obtains permission of his Platoon Commander, and then applies direct to the Platoon Commander in the new district. On transfer a man takes with him the whole of his personal equipment, and the appropriate accounting is carried out by the T. A. Associations involved.

Discharges

Discharges: The competent authority to authorize discharge of all ranks below Warrant Officer Class I is the Battalion Commander. In the case of Warrant Officers Class I the Zone Commander is the competent authority.

Documents and Records

Documents and Records: The only record maintained in respect of each volunteer is the enrollment form on which is also recorded casualties. When a volunteer's enrollment form is completed the Company Commander makes such extracts therefrom as are necessary for his Company Book. He then forwards the form to the local T. A. Association. In the case of a company being disbanded the Company Commander forwards his Company Book to the local T. A. Association.

Identity Card

There is issued to each member of the Home Guard an endorsement on his National Registration Identity Card showing that he is a member of that force. This document all members of the Home Guard must have on their persons at all times. This card permits the member of the Home Guard, when engaged in essential war service, uninterrupted passage through the various controls over movement on the public highways, etc.

Periodic Orders

Periodic Orders: Periodically, but at no set dates Company Commanders send to Battalion Commanders who transmit them to T. A. Associations orders known as Part II Orders. The following information is included in these orders:

Discharges, Transfers, Promotions or Reversions, Casualties, Extensions of Service over the age limit, Appointments to Commission, Special Instances of Gallant Conduct, etc.

Casualties

Casualties: A member of the Home Guard who sustains a wound or injury in the course of his duties at once reports the matter through his Section Commander and channels to his Battalion Commander.

The Battalion Commander is responsible for the completion of a detailed statement which he certifies and forwards to the T. A. Association where it is attached to the volunteer's enrollment form. The T. A. Associations notify the War Office of the killed and wounded during operations. They keep a record of the killed and wounded and of admissions to hospitals from duty.

Medical

Medical Attendance and Hospital Treatment: The British Medical Association has arranged through the T. A. Associations for local civilian medical practitioners to provide free of cost initial first aid treatment for casualties occurring to members of the Home Guard while on duty.

While in receipt of temporary disablement allowance (which will be referred to later) a member of the Home Guard may receive medical attendance from army sources, or hospital treatment in military hospitals and in certain cases in civil hospitals.

Discipline

Discipline: The Home Guard is part of the Armed Forces of the Crown and consequently its members are under the Army Act subject to military law and liable to obey such orders as are given to them in accordance with instructions issued by the Army Council. Summary punishments are not awarded to members of the Home Guard. If a volunteer proves himself to be not amenable to discipline or negligent in the discharge of his duties, he is discharged. In the event, however, of a volunteer committing an offence under the Army Act of so grave a nature that it cannot adequately be met by discharge the case is referred to higher regular army military authorities.

Complaints

Complaints: Complaints must be made to the immediate Unit Commander. If the Unit Commander cannot handle them they are passed up through the regular channels to the Commander who can. In no circumstances does a volunteer communicate direct with the War Office.

Press Communications

Press Communications: Members of the Home Guard who give anything to the Press must inform their superior officers that they are doing so. The members themselves are responsible that their communications to the Press are consistent with the requirements of security and discipline.

Inventions

Inventions: All members of the Home Guard inventing new military equipment or modifications of existing equipment must refer these inventions to the War Office. In no case are Unit Commanders authorized to try any new inventions without first obtaining War Office sanction.

Adjutant-Quartermaster Officers

Adjutant-Quartermaster Officers: Regular Army Officers having the acting rank of Captain are appointed to each Battalion of the Home Guard of a strength of 1,000 or over to perform the combined duties of Adjutant and Quartermaster. These appointments are made by the War Office. In certain cases the War Office will appoint one of these officers for Battalions having a strength of less than 1,000, but in most cases such Battalions have an Administrative Assistant, who is a civilian employed and paid by the T. A. Association, to do the same work. Battalions with a strength of 2,500 or over have both an A/Q Officer and an Administrative Assistant.

Administrative Assistants

Administrative Assistants: Paid Administrative Assistants who are civilians and are not enrolled in the Home Guard are appointed by the T. A. Associations to Group and Zone Commanders and to Battalions as mentioned above. The duty of these Administrative Assistants is to assist the Commanders with the general work of administration, more particularly in those aspects for which the T. A. Associations are generally responsible. The provision for Administartive Assistants originally covered Battalions and they were appointed to most Battalions. Since the authorization for A/Q Officers these officers have in most Battalions taken the place of Administrative Assistants (see above), but in certain Battalions it was found difficult to obtain the proper type of officer, so for the time being, April 1, 1940, at least, these Battalions have been permitted by the War Office to retain their Administrative Assistants.

Clerical Assistants

Clerical Assistants: All Home Guard Commanders are authorized to use voluntary clerical assistants, both male and female. Many women are helping in the different command offices. These volunteer clerical helpers are not enrolled in the Home Guard.

Permanent Staff Instructors

Permanent Staff Instructors: Regular Army Warrant Officers and Sergeants are appointed "Permanent Staff Instructors" (P.S.I.'s) for the Home Guard. Each Army Command Headquarters has a pool of such Instructors. The members of this pool circulate among the Units of the Home Guard in their Command. There are also posted a Permanent Staff Instructor to each Battalion and each Unit guarding a Public Utility Company. There is a Permanent Staff Instructor for about every six Battalions whose duty it is to deal with scattered units.

Telephones

Telephones: Where circumstances justify its installation one telephone is provided for every Home Guard Headquarters down to and including Company Headquarters. This telephone is connected to the nearest General Post Office exchange.

Financial Grant

Financial Grant: To meet expenditure for the Home Guard to the extent to which it fails to be defrayed by T. A. Associations' grants, a special grant was originally made to the Associations at the rate of 1£ for each man on the strength of Home Guard Units handled by those Associations on the 30th of June 1940. This was tentative and was to cover the organization expenses. Sir Edward Grigg stated as long ago as last November (1940) in the House of Commons that later proper and sufficient financing would be provided, but up to the 1st of April (1941) no official standard provision had been made.

Uniform Equipment

Uniform, Equipment, etc.: The following items are issued to each volunteer:

1. Suit of battle dress (the battle dress is the campaign uniform of the regular forces)
2. 1 Service respirator (gas mask)
3. 2 Eyeshields (these are anti-gas)
4. 1 Outfit of anti-gas ointment
5. 1 Steel helmet
6. 1 Field dressing
7. 1 Field service cap
8. 1 Greatcoat
9. 1 Pair of boots
10. 1 Pair of gaiters
11. 1 Belt
12. 1 Haversack
13. 2 "Home Guard" arm insignia
14. 1 Blanket for every two men, 1 ground sheet for every four men.

NOTE: It is to be remembered that the Home Guard works in shifts and consequently the latter two items serve the different shifts.

Members of the Home Guard are permitted to wear their decorations, service ribbons, etc. They have in fact in certain cases been decorated for their services in the Home Guard.

A member of the Home Guard on being "called up" for military service retains those items of dress and equipment which are common to the Regular Army and the Home Guard, which includes the uniform.

Home Guard Officers dress in the battle dress, that is, in the same uniform as the members of the force who are not commissioned.

Insignia of Rank

Insignia of Rank: Warrant Officers and Non-Commissioned Officers wear the same chevrons as the Regular Army. Commissioned Officers wear the same insignia of rank on their shoulder straps as the Regular Army.

Arms and Ammunition

Arms and Ammunition: The allotment of arms and ammunition for the Home Guard to the Army Commands is controlled by the Commander-in-Chief, Home Forces. The Army Commands sub-allot the arms and ammunition to Military Area Commanders, who in turn sub-allot to Zone, Group and Battalion. The Military Area Commanders are responsible for the storage of arms and ammunition. The actual supply of arms and ammunition as distinguished from its allotment is made from the regular army ordnance depots direct to the T. A. Associations which in turn issue to the Units. All arms issued are signed for by the Company or Sub-Unit Commander.

The general laws, rulings, etc. restricting ordinary citizens from having in their possession fire arms and ammunition do not apply to Members of the Home Guard because they are in His Majesty's Service.

Engineer and Ordnance Stores

Engineer and Ordnance Stores: The T. A. Associations are the normal channel of supply of Engineer and Ordnance Stores. These they obtain from regular army sources. Sometimes the T. A. Associations are authorized to make local purchases of small amounts of such stores. The T. A. Associations obtain or purchase such stores on the authority of the Military Area Commander.

Accounting

System of Accounting for Clothing, Arms and Stores: Clothing, Arms, Ammunition and Engineer and Ordnance Stores are vouchered by the Regular Army source to the T. A. Associations which maintain records of receipts and issues made to the Home Guard Units. The Associations obtain receipts from the Units and the Units in turn obtain receipts from each volunteer for articles issued to him.

Offices, Drill Halls, etc.

Accommodation—Provision of Offices, Drill Halls, etc.: The providing of premises for all purposes for the Home Guard is handled by the T. A. Associations. The Home Guard is authorized to accept voluntary offers of accommodation and, if necessary, space can be requisitioned through the proper Regular Army authorities.

Travel Allowances

Travel Allowances: Traveling expenses are allowed for authorized duty journeys. In addition to rail, bus, etc., private motor vehicles are used by the Home Guard members on duty. Motor mileage allowance is allowed in such cases (full details in our Main Report).

No one in Great Britain can purchase gasoline except with coupons which are officially issued. This is the machinery for rationing gasoline. Members of the Home Guard who are using their cars for Home Guard purposes purchase gasoline in the ordinary manner from garages, filling stations, etc. The necessary coupons to enable such purchases are provided by the T. A. Associations. Home Guard Commanders requisition as required on the T. A. Associations and are responsible for the issue and custody of such coupons. These Commanders maintain a record of receipts and issue of these coupons and account monthly to the T. A. Associations. Each coupon issued has the registration number of the vehicle concerned entered thereon.

Motor launches may be used by members of the Home Guard when necessary in the same way as private automobiles. The allowance in such case is the actual cost of the gasoline and oil used.

Use of Unlicensed Cars

Use of Unlicensed Cars: Due to the rationing of gasoline and the high license fee many automobiles are off the road in Great Britain. As a result there has been in certain localities a shortage of cars necessary for Home Guard purposes. These unlicensed cars are, of course, also uninsured. The Army Council has authorized the Military Area Commanders, where they consider it essential, to issue certificates authorizing the use of unlicensed and uninsured cars strictly for Home Guard purposes. These certificates are issued only to persons of responsibility and are withdrawn immediately in the event of any abuse. The insurance risk, apart from damage by enemy action (which we will speak of below) is borne by the War Office. Mileage allowance is allowed to the owners of these cars. This mileage allowance is less than that for the use of licensed cars because the insurance factor is eliminated from the allowance. Normal maintenance, repairs and garaging is the responsibility of the owner.

Automobile Insurance

Insurance of Privately Owned Motor Vehicles Used for Home Guard Purposes: The War Office has made an agreement with the Insurance Companies relative to the coverage on privately owned cars while being used for Home Guard purposes. This agreement provides that all current insurance policies covering use of cars on the road will cover driving and use by any person for the purposes of the Home Guard. This automatic extension does not extend the liability to cover those risks which are excluded by the War Risks Exclusion Clause. This last type of damage is to be dealt with under the general government scheme of compensation for War damage (see below). There is one exception to this. When the damage or loss occurs during emergency use, which means the use of the vehicle necessitated by enemy activity, it is compensated for out of Army funds.

Subsistence

Subsistence (Rations, Ration Allowance, etc.): Normally the Home Guard is fed at home. In certain cases where the Home Guard are unable to provide their own food, they are fed by a Regular Army Unit, if there is one close enough, but where the Home Guard is isolated they must set up their own feeding arrangement and for this purpose they are furnished with supplies in kind.

When we were in England it had been determined to issue to all Home Guard Units three to five days "iron rations" and the Directorate was working on the problem of distribution.

Where extra expense is necessarily incurred by the volunteer for food in the performance of his duties he is eligible for subsistence allowance. If he is employed on a continuous period of duty in excess of five hours, but not more than ten hours, subsistence allowance may be claimed at the rate of 1s 6d. Where the period is in excess of ten hours at the rate of 3s.

Disablement Allowance

Temporary (Total or Partial) Disablement Allowance While Still a Member of the Home Guard: If the temporary disability is total for the time being allowances are paid at a basic rate of 35s a week, with certain additions for a wife and children. If during the period of total disablement the volunteer is in receipt of free hospital treatment, a deduction of 10s a week is made from the allowance. The addition for a wife is also payable if the wife is separated, but was married to the volunteer before the date of the disablement. This addition also covers an unmarried dependent living as a wife. The addition for children covers legitimate, legitimated, adopted, stepchildren and illegitimate children who are being regularly maintained by a volunteer. The addition for children is payable for children up to 16 years of age, except where an older child is receiving only nominal wages or is being educated at a university, technical or secondary school, or is incapable of self-support and has not reached the age of 21 years.

If the temporary disability is only partial the allowance to the member varies according to the degree of disablement from a basic weekly allowance of 34s 2d to 6s 10d.

Allowances may be granted to the family of a member of the Home Guard who is either totally or partially disabled and is receiving a disability allowance as above. This family allowance varies proportionally with the degree of the volunteer's disablement. The maximum allowance for a wife is 8s 4d; for the first child when there is a wife, 6s 3d, and for each further child 5s. If no allowance is being paid for a wife, for the first child 8s 4d, the second child 6s 3d, and any additional children 5s. The degree of disablement is expressed as a percentage of complete disablement and this percentage is applied to the allowance. Allowances for children terminate as above at the age of 16 with the same exceptions as outlined above. In case of government employees disablement allowance is not paid in addition to equivalent sick pay.

The regulations governing the claiming and payment of the above allowances are issued by the Army Council. These regulations provide the machinery for the claiming and handling of the disability allowances. They are covered by special Army Order 111, 1940.

Pensions

Pensions: Permanent or continuing disablement after discharge from the force are dealt with by the Ministry of Pensions under the War Pensions Warrant, 1940. The disability must be attributable to military service during this War. The claim must be made within seven years from the termination of service, or at the end of the War, whichever is earlier. The rate of pension varies according to the degree of disablement. The various degrees are assessed as a certain percentage of total disablement. The weekly rates of pension vary from 34s 2d for 100% to 6s 10d for 20%. Gratuities are also payable for certain minor injuries, such as the loss of fingers, toes, etc. In addition in case of total disablement an allowance up to 15s a week may be granted if the constant and continuous attendance of a nurse or other attendant is necessary. Family allowances may be granted to the family of a volunteer who is receiving a disability pension as outlined above.

Pensions to Widows

Pensions to Widows: The widow of a member of the Home Guard is paid a pension if his death was caused by the War. The rates of widow's pensions are as follows: (1) If she has a child or children entitled to allowances, or is over 40 years of age, or is incapable of supporting herself, at the rate of 22s 6d a week; (2) if she is under 40 and without children 15s 6d a week. Under certain conditions a wife who was separated from her husband is entitled to a widow's pension. The pension of a widow or separated wife ceases on her re-marriage, but the allowance for children (see below) may continue to be paid. Under certain conditions an unmarried dependent who was living as a wife may be paid a pension of not more than 10s a week.

Children's Pensions and Allowances

Children's Pensions and Allowances: A widow or separated wife who is receiving a pension may be granted a weekly allowance for each child under 16 maintained by her. The rates of allowance are for the first child 8s 6d, for the second child 6s 3d, for additional children 5s each. An unmarried dependent who was living as a wife may be granted the same allowances for children which she maintains. Children under 16 of a deceased member of the Home Guard who are motherless may be paid a pension at the rate of 10s a week. Pensions may be paid to the parents of a deceased member of the Home Guard if they are in pecuniary need arising from old age or infirmity. If no other pension or allowance has been granted, pensions may be granted to a grandfather, grandmother, step-father, step-mother, grandson, grand-daughter, brother (including a half-brother), sister (including a half-sister), or a person who acted as a parent and wholly supported the deceased during his childhood for not less than 5 years, under certain conditions. Only one person can receive a pension under this heading.

Life Insurance

Life Insurance Policies: Many of the life policies issued in England contain a clause requiring extra premiums if the holder serves in the Crown Forces. The companies have agreed to waive this clause so long as the Home Guard remain voluntary, unpaid and serve only at home.

Maintenance of Families

Maintenance of Families: While normally under the Home Guard scheme volunteers will not be absent from their homes and work and will consequently be able to look after and support their families, it is conceivable that circumstances may arise, e.g. in the event of invasion, when they may not be able to support their families for an extended period. In such case the families, if they are in need, will be eligible for immediate assistance under the Government scheme for the prevention and relief of distress caused by the War. This scheme is administered by the Assistance Board. The War Office has announced that there is no question of any stigma attaching to the receipt of payments from the Assistance Board. It has stated that any disorganization caused by invasion and consequent distress among the civilian population is not likely to be confined to the families of the Home Guard and the arrangements made by the Assistance Board will cover civilians generally who need assistance in any area affected during a period of emergency.

Funeral Expenses

Funeral Expenses: The funeral expenses for members of the Home Guard who die while on duty or because of injury, etc., resulting from duty are paid by the military authorities, or refunded to the relatives up to a limit of £7 10s.

General Government Scheme of Compensation for War Damage

General Government Scheme of Compensation for War Damage: The British Government has been working on a general scheme to compensate for war damage. We were told that this scheme contemplated no settlement for such damage until after the end of the war. We believe that since we left England a bill to implement this scheme has been introduced into Parliament and passed. We do not have a copy of the bill available.

Part Four—Pitfalls and Conclusions

Section I—Pitfalls

It seemed advisable to us that not only should we study the accomplishments of the British Home Guard, but that we should as well inform ourselves of the pitfalls which have been encountered in its organization and administration. The British themselves are fully conversant with the problems they have met and the mistakes they have made in organizing the Home Guard, and it was with these in mind that all of those who have been responsible emphasized,—"All of the forces entering into the defense of a country should be planned from the very beginning, so that they will coordinate and be integrated into the plan as a whole." (Words of General Sir Alan Brooke.)

It is almost impossible in a Summary Report to summarize intelligently the pitfalls and problems, which are in themselves necessarily individual. Our Main Report will deal with them at length. However, we shall enumerate without detail in the Summary Report some of the basic pitfalls.

1. In the early summer of 1939 Great Britain had its Army, had its Navy, had its Air Force and to some degree, its Civilian Defence Forces. Following the outbreak of the war every possible effort was bent towards strengthening those forces and developing methods of cooperation that would in turn put Great Britain in a more powerful position. It was not, however, until early in May 1940, long after the war had started, that the need of a force such as the Home Guard was realized. It was not until May 14th that the Local Defense Volunteers (Home Guard) was organized. It is obvious that to bring into the plan of total defense at so late a date, a new force of 1,700,000 strength, involved substantial problems. The personnel problem was one of the difficulties resulting from the late planning and organization of the Home Guard. Many of the ablest men with former military experience, who should have been available for the organizing and officering of the Home Guard had already been used in the Civil Defence Forces. Either the Home Guard would be denied many men who were peculiarly fitted for service in that force or the Civil Defence Forces would lose many men who had helped, through their enthusiasm and personality, to build up those forces, who had received much training in the work of those forces, who knew their peculiar problems and who had been directing their activities. This would have been avoided if both forces had been planned and organized concurrently.

2. The founding of the Home Guard was very hasty and to meet an immediate emergency. The proper staff work had not been

done. The confusion which followed Mr. Anthony Eden's appeal on May 14th taught the lesson that fairly complete plans for the organization of such a force as the Home Guard should be prepared in advance.

This same confusion, finally resulting in July in the discontinuance of acceptance of volunteers for the Home Guard, indicated that a cadre of officers and non-commissioned officers should be enlisted or enrolled prior to the accepting of volunteers.

4. The immediate exigencies of the emergency at the time of the organization of the Home Guard resulted in its formation before any provision had been made for supplying it with equipment and weapons. Under the circumstances this was warranted, but it resulted in many difficulties including a dampening effect upon the spirits of the volunteers. It is a great tribute to the British that the morale of the force was not more affected. In the absence of such immediate necessity the British experience points to the advisability of planning for the supply of adequate euipment and arms for the force prior to its organization. For one thing, unless the force is properly uniformed, the government exposes its members to being treated as franc-tireurs.

5. As can be seen from this report Field Fortifications of various kinds enter importantly into the mission of the Home Guard. In Great Britain the lack of properly prepared and designed type plans for such construction and the lack of a proper understanding of the principles governing their siting resulted in much willing but inefficient work which had to be done over again.

6. In Britain the lack at the start of a clear understanding as to the proper relationship and coordination between different types of units within the Home Guard resulted in much bad feeling and waste of energy. By types of units is meant, for instance: Local Units; Factory Units; Railroad Units and Miscellaneous Units.

7. Lack at the beginning of the Home Guard Directorate in the War Office led to disorganization and inefficiency in the planning, organization and administration of the Home Guard.

8. The peculiar idea at the time of the organization of the Home Guard that there should be no rank in the organization resulted in many difficulties and was soon corrected so that today the officers hold King's Commissions.

9. The postponement of the organization of the Home Guard resulted, when it was formed, in the necessity of dealing with a group of sporadic local defence movements and organizations, and the difficulties of fitting them into a general scheme and coordinating them into a system of unified command.

Section J. Conclusions

SECTION J—*Conclusions.*

We find it even more difficult to summarize our conclusions many of which might be of some value, even if about minor points. We shall accordingly leave our completed conclusions for the "Main Report" and in this "Summary Report" deal only with the broader factors.

As we see it, the major issue before the American people today is as to whether this country is faced with possible danger from an outside enemy or not.

If there is no danger, then we should stop immediately our extensive plans for building up a war machine. If there is danger, it is our belief that we should consider most seriously the statement made to us on our arrival in England by General Lord Robert Bridgeman, namely, "There is little use of undertaking preparedness if we do not prepare for the possible worst, and the Home Guard is a very definite and vital part today in the defence of any country."

It is our belief that the American people are almost unanimous in their belief that this country should prepare for possible danger ahead.

As a result of our studies and conferences in England, not only with those men on whose shoulders rest the responsibility of the defence of that country, but with the official representatives and military officers of the invaded countries, we unqualifiedly believe that the Home Guard is just as vital and important an arm of the total defence of any country as any of the other forces, such as the Army and Navy and the Civil Defence Forces.

We all know of the new infiltration tactics of the enemy, with their amazing cooperative use of tanks, airplanes, air-borne troops, and Fifth Columnists, and of the havoc, destruction and panic wrought far into the unprotected areas of the front lines of the invaded countries.

We now ask this question.
Is there today in this country any military force locally organized "in depth" back of our borders and coastlines—a special force whose duty it is to warn, to delay and to harrass the enemy, in event of an invasion, in whatever place they may initiate a surprise attack?

Our answer to that question is,—"No."

Yet, it is just those areas which have been most vulnerable to enemy attack from which they have carried on their amazingly efficient, cooperative action, resulting in such confusion and disorganization that resistance has collapsed.

It is submitted that the experience on the continent has shown that the answer to this form of attack is such a force as the British Home Guard, which will reduce to the minimum the surprise effect of the enemy attack, and retard him so that the active regular forces can deliver their counter-attack.

The public might readily ask,—

"Why not have these areas defended by the regular forces or by full-time soldiers?"

There are several answers to that question.

In the first place, it would require a tremendously large body of men who must be spotted all through such areas in small units. Where then, if the regular troops are used for such purposes, would there be any large concentrated force with the power to strike back.

The question might further be asked,—

"Why not increase the regular army over and above its ordinary requirements to the extent necessary to do this job?"

In the first place, it would be a financial burden that the country could not stand.

In the second place, and what is even more important, the productive capacity and economic set-up of the country would be seriously and dangerously interfered with by the withdrawing of so many men from productive occupations.

There is just one answer to that type of offence. It is a Home Guard composed of volunteers carrying on their civilian jobs and at the same time prepared to play their part in the military defence of their country.

NOTE: It has been officially stated in England that:
"The cost of administering the Home Guard adequately and efficiently for one year is about equal to the cost of running the whole war for six hours."

The public may further ask: "What need is there of such a force against invasion? Will an enemy ever attempt to invade us? How could an enemy invade us? How an enemy might invade, or, when an enemy might invade cannot today be answered. Perhaps those questions never will be answered, but there are few people in existence today who conceived in 1939 that the Germans could accomplish what they have by July, 1941. There is no one who can definitely forecast the future. There are but few who dare hazard conclusions on the development of science. We believe that there is no one who can prophesy accurately what position South America may be in if Germany gains complete control of the Eastern Hemisphere with Africa less than two thousand miles away.

Once the control of an ocean is gone, it becomes a highway for invasion rather than a moat for defence. There are various contingencies which are not entirely without the realm of possibility and in which the combined British and American control of the seas would be lost. In the case of some great disaster to Great Britain, how can we foretell how much of the British Fleet would be left. Is it not possible that a situation might come about where it was a question of building capacity. We understand that the experts believe that under such circumstances an Axis-controlled Europe together with Japan could ultimately outbuild the United States and Canada. Under such circumstances, we would be sorry if we had not done everything possible to prepare this country against possible invasion.

In September of 1939 the Germans used parachutes to land troops and agents in a comparatively small way in their conquest of Poland. In April 1940 they startled the world by their use of air-borne troops in Norway and in May of 1940 to an even greater extent in Holland. In May of 1941 they invaded and conquered the Island of Crete by practically the sole use of air troops. We understand that there were about 50,000 British and allied troops in Crete. Is it not fair to assume that the Germans used at least as many air-borne troops in the operation? While we were in England in March, we were told that the Germans had four trained air-borne divisions in addition to their parachute troops. Perhaps it is a far cry to visualizing an air invasion of this country, but who can say where the development of air transport as applied to military operations is leading? We must remember that the range of our largest bombers today is about 3000 miles and that it is estimated to be nearly 7000 for our experimental B-19.

We are confident that there is no one who can deny the need of a force similar to the Home Guard as a part of the defence of England or that it would have been of incalculable importance to the invaded and conquered countries.

If it is deemed that such a force may ever be a wise and necessary part of the defence preparation of the United States, it is our belief that comprehensive plans and the necessary staff work should be undertaken at once, rather than wait for a more imminent emergency, thus avoiding the confusion and inefficiency experienced in England. Even today there are sporadic movements resulting in the organization of home-defence units in various localities. Individual States may start individual movements. We hold no brief against the spirit of such patriotic endeavors. However, in the event of an increased threat of invasion, the Home Guard with its military function must act in cooperation with the "regular" forces under a unified command. If the Home Guard is not included from the beginning in a planned system of defence, it is obvious that to achieve its proper integration in the system will be difficult. It is evident then that one intelligently conceived plan for "the whole" must come from some central source. If there is no general plan prepared by a central source, it is conceivable that the 48 States might have 48 different plans, to say nothing of locally interjected sporadic movements which would complicate the problem still more. In the event of invasion, or an imminent threat of invasion, our Commander-in-Chief would be seriously handicapped.

There should be worked out one intelligent workable plan adaptable to any State and available to all States. A State accepting such a plan could organize within the State and be prepared to be taken over on order of the proper Federal authority in the event of invasion or increased threat.

England's unfortunate experience in the lack of a Home Guard Directorate in the War Office for sometime after the Home Guard was formed, as explained in paragraphs above, leads us to the very definite conclusion that the formation of a similar Directorate or Bureau in the War Department should be undertaken at the outset. It is obvious that a force such as the British Home Guard for this country would be very large. The very size of such a force indicates the necessity for a special Bureau in the War Department, properly staffed.

In conclusion, we certainly are not immune from the German weapons of sabotage and espionage—the Fifth Columnists. How better can a country be protected against these weapons than to have a force whose primary purpose is the protection of its country, and which reaches into every City, Town and Village, into every home, office and plant?

England, of all the countries attacked so far, is the only one which has been united and is the only one which has survived. What greater single force to unite this country than a voluntary organization of men drawn from every station and occupation in life—all working together for the safety of their country?

Bibliography

Bibliography:

The following is a list of books, pamphlets, and other printed data which we have studied and referred to in the preparation of our reports (Summary Report and Main Report). Our work has included as well an examination into some of the back files of the English newspapers, including The London Times, The Daily Mirror, The Evening Standard, The Christian Science Monitor, The Daily Express, The Evening News, The London Illustrated News, The Manchester Guardian, etc.

Most of our material bears the stamp of His Majesty's Government or is issued officially by the War Department. Some of the material is semi-official being recommended by the War Office. All other material has been recommended to us personally by officials who we believe to be experts in their line. A considerable portion of all this material will be used as exhibits in our Main Report.

"Home Guard for Victory" by Hugh Slater
"The First Quarter" by Sir Ronald Storrs
"The Third Quarter" by Philip Graves
"The Fourth Quarter" by Philip Graves
"China's Struggle with the Dictators" by O. M. Greene
"The Story of Poland" by Bernard Newman
"The German Fifth Column in Poland" — published by the Polish Ministry of Information
"I Saw It Happen in Norway" by Carl Hambro, President of Norwegian Parliament
"The Rape of the Netherlands" by E. N. van Kleffens
"Parachutes Over Holland" by Leonard Moseley
"General deGaulle (The Hope of France)" by Gallicus
"Death to the French" by C. S. Forrester
"The Road to Bordeaux" by Freeman and Cooper
"Tragedy in France" by Andre Maurois
"The Truth About France" by Louis Levy
"The Army of the Future" by deGaulle
"The War for World Power" by Strategicus
"Armies of Freemen" by Wintringham
"New Ways of War" by Wintringham
"Freedom of Our Weapons" by Wintringham
"The Home Guard Can Fight" by Wintringham
"How to Fight" by Pilling
"Home Guard Pocketbook" by General A. F. U. Greene

"Home Guard Handbook" by Brophy

"Home Guard Drill Book and Field Service Manual" by Brophy

"The Home Guard Training Manual" by Langdon-Davies

"Dynamic Defense" by Liddell Hart

"The Gun" by C. S. Forrester

"Home Guard Training" by Colonel H. S. Levy

"The Spotter's Handbook" by Francis Chichester

"Battle Training—Parts I, II and III" by General Rowan-Robinson and Colonel H. A. Pollock

"Hints for the Home Guard" by Colonel Fitzwilliams

"The Wounded Don't Cry" by Quentin Reynolds

"Aircraft Recognition" by Saville-Sneath

"Anti-Aircraft Defense"— issued by Military Service Publishing Company

"Rights and Powers of the Home Guard" by John Burke

"Drill Up-To-Date"—issued by Longmans, Greene and Company

"The Diary of a Staff Officer"

"Defence Regulations Seventh Edition January 1941"

"King's Regulations for the Army 1940"

"Emergency Powers (Defence) Act 1939"

"National Service (Armed Forces) Act 1939"

"National Service (Armed Forces) Act 1940"

"The Army Act of 1881 Amended to 1940"

"Armed Forces (Conditions of Service) Act 1939"

"National Registration Act 1939"

"Regulations for the Allowances of the Army 1938"

"Court (Emergency Powers) Amendment Act 1940"

"Royal Warrant Retired Pay and Pensions, etc."

"Proposed War Damage Bill" (Tentative Draft)

"Military Lands Act 1892 and Amendment 1903"

"1938-1939 Public General Acts"

"Generals and Generalship" by General Wavell (Pamphlet)

"Anthony Eden's Broadcast May 14th, 1940"

"Parliamentary Debates House of Commons
    May 22, 1940
    November 5, 1940
    November 6, 1940
    November 19, 1940"

"History of the Home Guard"—Typewritten Copy by Captain Ryley, Home Guard Directorate

"The Home Guard Keeps Watch"—Article by General T. R. Eastwood

"Suggestions for Battalion Commanders"—written by a Commander of one of the Home Guard Units

"Plan of an Industrial Factory Doing Some War Work and Memorandum Showing Plans of the Evacuation of a Factory"

"Some Remarks on Home Guard in Factories with List of Pitfalls"—written by Home Guard Factory Battalion Commander

"We also Serve"—Official Radio Broadcast

"Is The Home Guard an Answer to Norway, Holland, etc.?"—Broadcast by Colonel Morgan

"Set of Operational Orders for a Home Guard Zone"

"Pie"—a Publication by a Home Guard Zone

"Syllabus of Training, etc., of a Home Guard Zone School for Arms"

"Memorandum Regarding Strength of London District"

"Summary, Home Guard Formations"

"Notes of Lectures Given at the Home Guard Training School at Hurlingham" (Now abandoned)

Catalog—Defence Research Studio

"Manual of Elementary Drill (All Arms) 1935"

"Cadet Training 1938"

"Signal Training (All Arms) 1938 and Amendment No. 1"

"Notes on Map Reading (And Amendments 1-4 1939)"

"Medical Manual of Chemical Warfare 1940"

"Vocabulary of German Military Terms"

"Infantry Training (Training in War 1937)"

"Infantry Training (Section Leading 1938)"

"Infantry Training 1937 supplement 1941—(Tactical Notes for Platoon Commanders)"

"Army Training Memoranda No. 33 (War) June 1940"

Army Training Memoranda No. 34 (War) July 1940

Army Training Memoranda No. 35 (War) August 1940

Army Training Memoranda No. 36 (War) September 1940

Army Training Memoranda No. 37 1940

Army Training Memoranda No. 38 1941

M. T. P. (Military Training Pamphlet):

M. T. P. No. 21—Dannert Concertina Wire Obstacles

M. T. P. No. 21 A 1939—Construction of Dannert Concertina Wire Obstacles

M. T. P. No. 21 B 1939—Dannert Concertina Wire Instructions for Closing and Fastening

M. T. P. No. 23—Operations Part I, Supplement 1939—Particulars of Artillery and Small Arms Weapons, Bridges and Fords

M. T. P. No. 23—Operations Part IV 1939—Protection
M. T. P. No. 23—Operations Part V 1940—The Use of Gas in the Field
M. T. P. No. 24 1939—Training of Motorcyclists
M. T. P. No. 26 1939—Notes on Concealment and Camouflage
M. T. P. No. 30—Field Engineering (All Arms) Part II Notes on Screens
M. T. P. No. 30—Field Engineering (All Arms) Part III Obstacles 1940
M. T. P. No. 32—The Tactical and Technical Employment of Chemical Weapons—Part VI, Bombs, Ground, Six Pound
M. T. P. No. 33—1940 Training in Fieldcraft and Elementary Tactics
M. T. P. No. 34—Royal Armoured Corps Weapon Training—Part VII—Smoke—1940
M. T. P. No. 40—Anti-Tank Mines—1940
M. T. P. No. 42—Tank Hunting and Destruction—1940 and Amendments Nos. 1 and 2 (Plans of Northover Projector).
M. T. P. No. 45—Bomb Reconnaissance and Protection Against Unexploded Bombs (All Arms).
S. A. T. (Small Arms Training):
S. A. T. Vol. 1, Pamphlet 1—Weapon Training and Amendments
S. A. T. Vol. 1, Pamphlet 2—Application of Fire and Amendments
S. A. T. Vol. 1, Pamphlet 3—Rifle and Amendments
S. A. T. Vol. 1, Pamphlet 5—Anti-Tank Rifle and Amendment
S. A. T. Vol. 1, Pamphlet 6—Anti-Aircraft and Amendments
S. A. T. Vol. 1, Pamphlet 7, Part I—.303 Machine Guns—Mechanical Subjects
S. A. T. Vol. 1, Pamphlet 7, Part II—.303 Machine Gun Training
S. A. T. Vol. 1, Pamphlet 7, Part III—.303 Machine Gun—Fire Control
S. A. T. Vol. 1, Pamphlet 7, Supplement—.303 Machine Gun
S. A. T. Vol. 1, Pamphlet 11—Pistols
S. A. T. Vol. 1, Pamphlet 12—Bayonet
S. A. T. Vol. 1, Pamphlet 13—Grenade
S. A. T. Vol. 1, Pamphlet 13—Supplement
S. A. T. Vol. 1, Pamphlet 20—.303 Lewis Machine Gun
S. A. T. Vol. 1, Pamphlet 21—Thompson Machine Gun
Pocket Notes on Identification of German Units
Instructional Notes on the .300 inch Browning Automatic Rifle, 1940
Instructional Notes on the Ross Rifle .303 Mark III B, 1940
Instructional Notes on the Lewis Machine Gun (Ground Action, 1940)

Field Service Pocket Book Pamphlet 1, 1940—Glossary of Military Terms and Organization in the Field.
Field Service Pocket Book Pamphlet 2—Orders—1939
Field Service Pocket Book Pamphlet 3—Intelligence—1939
Field Service Pocket Book Pamphlet 4—Field Engineers—1939
Field Service Pocket Book Pamphlet 5—Billets, Camps and Bivouacs—1939
Field Service Pocket Book Pamphlet 8—Protection Against Gas—1939
Field Service Pocket Book Pamphlet 9—Supply, etc.—1939
Field Service Pocket Book Pamphlet 10—Medical Sources—1939
Field Engineering Pamphlet 9—1941—Booby and Tank Traps
L. D. V. T. I. (Local Defence Volunteers Training Instructions)
L. D. V. T. I. No. 1—1940—Road Blocks—Defence of Villages
L. D. V. T. I. No. 2—1940—Role and Status
L. D. V. T. I. No. 3—1940—German Parachute Troops
L. D. V. T. I. No. 4—1940—Training
L. D. V. T. I. No. 5—1940—Elements of Training
L. D. V. T. I. No. 6—1940—Relations Between Civil Defence Services and L.D.V.s.
L. D. V. T. I. No. 7—1940—Notes on Field Defences
L. D. V. T. I. No. 8—1940—Tanks and Tank Destruction
L. D. V. T. I. No. 9—1940—Grenades
H. G. I. (Home Guard Instruction)
H. G. I. No. 10—1940—General Instructions
H. G. I. No. 11—1940—Miscellaneous Notes
H. G. I. No. 12—1940—Factory Defence
H. G. I. No. 13—1940—Drill
H. G. I. No. 14—1940—Winter Training
H. G. I. No. 15—1940—Common German Military Expressions
H. G. I. No. 16—1940—Siting and Zeroing
H. G. I. No. 17—1940—Anti-Aircraft Training
H. G. I. No. 18—1940—Care and Cleaning of Weapons
H. G. I. No. 19—1940—Sentries
H. G. I. No. 20—1940—Documents
H. G. I. No. 21—1940—Indoor Tactical Training
H. G. I. No. 22—1940—Guides
H. G. I. No. 23—1941—Night Training
H. G. I. No. 24—1941—Protection Against Gas
H. G. I. No. 26—1941—Miscellaneous Notes
A. C. I. (Army Council Instructions)
A. C. I. Nos. 241, 242, 243—1940—Sentries—1940

A. C. I. Nos. 628—639—Miscellaneous—1940
A. C. I. No. 653—Local Defence Volunteers—1940
A. C. I. No. 751—778—Allowances, etc.—1940
A. C. I. No. 924—The Home Guard—1940
A. C. I. Nos. 1138—1161—Miscellaneous—September, 1940
A. C. I. Nos. 1206—1229—Miscellaneous—October, 1940
A. C. I. Nos. 1350—1366—Miscellaneous—1940
A. C. I. Nos. 1481—1492—Miscellaneous—1940
A. C. I. Nos. 1533—1544—Miscellaneous—1940
A. C. I. No. 1545—Miscellaneous—1940
A. C. I. No. 1563—Miscellaneous—1940
A. C. I. Nos. 1582 and 1583—Miscellaneous—1940
A. C. I. Nos. 114—116—Miscellaneous—1941
A. C. I. Nos. 192 and 193—Miscellaneous—1941
A. C. I. Nos. 288—290—Miscellaneous—1941
Seventeen War Office Letters and Urgent Postal Telegrams on Special Information to be Conveyed to the Home Guard.
Army Form W 3066—Enrollment in Home Guard
S. R. & O. (Statutory Rules and Orders)
S. R. & O. No. 1099—National Service (Armed Forces) Prevention of Evasion Regulations
S. R. & O. No. 1248—National Registration—1939
S. R. & O. No. 1836— National Registration Amendment—1939
S. R. & O. No. 55 —Petroleum—1940
S. R. & O. No. 748 —Defence (L.D.V.) Regulations—1940
S. R. & O. No. 814 —National Registration Amendment—1940
S. R. & O. No. 941 —General Regulations—1940
S. R. & O. No. 962 —Petroleum—1940
S. R. & O. No. 1383—L. D. V. and Alternative Title The Home Guard—1940
S. R. & O. No. 1537—Prevention of Evasion Regulation Amendment—1940
S. R. & O. No. 1613—Special Enlistments—1940
S. R. & O. No. 2003—Commissions—1940
S. R. & O. No. 2017—Commissions—1940
S. R. & O. No. 68 —General Regulations—1941
S. R. & O. No. 186 —Commissions—1941
Notes for Instructors on Principles of Instruction
Provisional Rules and Orders—1940—Road Traffic and Vehicles—1939
Special Army Orders No. 111—1940—Royal Warrant—Disablement Allowances

C.R.F.N. 1/2660 (O.P.S.) Method of Halting Motorists—July, 1940
Outline of M.T.7 Personnel and Duties
"Notes on Financial Aspect of the Home Guard" by Colonel Morgan
O.I.C. (Orders in Council):
O.I.C. March, 1927—Basis of King's Commission
O.I.C. July, 1939—Regarding Army Council
Colored Landscape Charts for Study of Home Guard Tactics
"Armed for Defence" by Wintringham—reprint article from Picture Post
"Defence"—reprint from the Services Magazine
Sketches showing method of "Tree Trunk" Road Blocks
Posters—"Types of British Aircraft"
Posters—"How to Hit Back at Dive-Bombers—Part I and Part II."
Chart of the P-17 .300 Lee Enfield Rifle
100 Photographs taken at War Office School No. 1 (Personally taken).